WOMAN OF INFLUENCE

Ten Traits of Those Who Want to Make a Difference

PAM FARREL

InterVarsity Press
Downers Grove, Illinois

InterVarsity Press® is the book-publishing division of InterVarsity Christian Fellowship®, a student movement active on campus at hundreds of universities, colleges and schools of nursing in the United States of America, and a member movement of the International Fellowship of Evangelical Students. For information about local and regional activities, write Public Relations Dept., InterVarsity Christian Fellowship, 6400 Schroeder Rd., P.O. Box 7895, Madison, WI 53707-7895.

All Scripture quotations, unless otherwise indicated, are taken from the HOLY BIBLE, NEW INTERNATIONAL VERSION®. NIV®. Copyright ©1973, 1978, 1984 by International Bible Society. Used by permission of Zondervan Publishing House. All rights reserved.

Cover photograph: Sandy Roessler Clark/F. P. G. International

ISBN 0-8308-1951-7

Printed in the United States of America ♾

Library of Congress Cataloging-in-Publication Data

Farrel, Pam, 1959-
   Woman of influence: ten traits of those who want to make a
difference/Pam Farrel.
     p. cm.
   Includes bibliographical references.
   ISBN 0-8308-1951-7 (pbk.: alk. paper)
   1. Women in Christianity. 2. Christian leadership. 3. Women in
the Bible. I. Title.
BV639.W7F37 1996
248.8'43—dc20
                                            95-26745
                                             CIP

| 20 | 19 | 18 | 17 | 16 | 15 | 14 | 13 | 12 | 11 | 10 | 9 | 8 | 7 | 6 | 5 | 4 | 3 | 2 |
| 12 | 11 | 10 | 09 | 08 | 07 | 06 | 05 | 04 | 03 | 02 | 01 | 00 | 99 | 98 | 97 | 96 |

To my mother, Afton
Thank you for showing me the world through
your eyes. I gained compassion.

To my husband, Bill
Thank you for seeing me through
God's eyes. I gained courage.

Preface: Why Influence? —————— 7

1 A Woman of Influence Is Impassioned —————— 10
Finding Your Unique Calling

2 A Woman of Influence Is an Individual —————— 27
Discovering Your Leadership Style

3 A Woman of Influence Is Intimate with God —————— 46
Connecting with Your Creator

4 A Woman of Influence Is Idealistic —————— 64
Daring to Dream

5 A Woman of Influence Is Interdependent —————— 77
Sharpening Your People Skills

6 A Woman of Influence Takes Initiative —————— 94
Reaching Your Potential

7 A Woman of Influence Has Integrity —————— 112
Consistent Living in an Inconsistent World

8 A Woman of Influence Is Intense —————— 128
Staying Power for the Long Haul

9 A Woman of Influence Is Inquiring —————— 143
Getting Answers on How to Grow

10 A Woman of Influence Is Infectious —————— 157
Being a Contagious Christian

Discussion Questions —————— 174

Notes —————— 183

Preface

Why Influence?

A WOMAN IS WALKING ALONG THE BEACH. SHE SEES AN OLDER WOMAN picking up starfish and tossing them into the sea. The young woman, thinking the older woman's efforts futile, asks, "Old woman, why do you do that? There are so many starfish, and the sea's waves unceasingly beat up against the shore. You toss a few back, but what difference does it make?"

The old woman picks up a starfish, flings it into the ocean and says, "It made a difference to *that* one!"

For many years I studied the women in the Bible. I investigated their lives, looking for the ingredients that made them usable to God. Then I started observing contemporary women whose lives were making a difference in the world to which God had called them—government, religion, the arts, business, education, medicine, science, social service and the home. I noticed that certain character qualities were common among all these women. As I read biographies of women who have influenced history, similar character traits were evident in their lives.

My heart is aimed at equipping women to be all God intends them to be. And this book is my attempt to help you see the special path of influence God has carved for you.

Influence can be defined as *earning the right to be heard so that others are moved toward their best.* We are better equipped for influence if we develop the ten character qualities discussed in this book.

You may think, *Oh, no! Pack my bags, I'm going on a guilt trip. I can't be all these things.* This book is *not* about guilt; it's about growth. Influence is not perfection—it is life in process.

Measuring the full impact of influence is nearly impossible. When I was a little girl, I loved to pick the dandelions when they were fluffy and white. I'd blow, and hundreds of little helicopters would fly into the air. I tried to watch where they all went, but as they got caught in the breeze, many would blow higher and higher until they disappeared. Just like those seeds, influence often isn't noticed until it blossoms later in the garden of someone else's life. Our words and actions may land close to home, or they may be carried far and wide.

You may make a difference—a significant difference in the life of another. Certain women of influence are woven as strands of strength in my own life. Their words form a pattern of hope on my heart.

My mother told me from early on, "Pam, be a leader." I can hear her whispers, even now during my darkest days, "You can do it. Just try. You'll see. I know you can." She sacrificed tremendously to ensure that I gained wings to fly.

My grandmother's words, spoken during dishwashing conversations, always remind me of my purpose: "Pam, share your talent." Then she would take me to a nursing home where I would do gymnastics for the patients and pass out fruit and kind words. My talent was just ordinary, but when it was connected to a purpose, I felt extraordinary.

My sister, Deney, was my treasured best friend through our years growing up. Night after night we whispered hopes and dreams in the comfortable shadows of our cozy room.

Kathy Hansell and her eight-year-old daughter, Kelly, let me play in their front yard and encouraged my family to go to church. That influence eventually led me into the Bible, where I met Jesus personally.

In college, Tina Wilcox, a young newlywed on staff with Campus Crusade for Christ, taught me about growing in my walk with God. My courageous peers in the group, Grace, Cindy and Debbie, encouraged me to walk the new life.

In seminary, Phoebe O'Neal taught me graciousness and hospitality and instilled in me a deeper hunger to reach the lost. Karen Dirks prayed for me and encouraged me to be myself. Sally Conway believed God had a calling on my life. She and her husband, Jim, entrusted their names to us on the cover of the book my husband and I wrote with them (*Pure Pleasure: Making Your Marriage a Great Affair*, IVP). Sally has strengthened me with her time, her wisdom and her talent.

During the writing of this book, Ruth Tucker was especially encouraging. My kindred friends involved with women's ministry also held me up with their prayers. Many other women, too numerous to name, have buoyed me up in times of weariness and stress. Each friend was important. Some will be on the pages of this book, but all are on the pages of my heart. Their words have seasoned my life. Influence, just like salt shaken out, is hard to see, but its flavor is hard to miss.

These women had no way of knowing how God was using them. You may feel that same way. You want to be used but have no idea how. Or you feel God has given you a platform to make a difference and you want to make the best use of it. It is my prayer that within the pages of this book you will discover the hope, strength and encouragement to be a "woman of influence" within your world.

The shores of your life are covered with starfish. Make a difference. Turn the page and begin your journey of influence.

Chapter 1

A Woman
of Influence
Is Impassioned

INDIA WAS THE LAST PLACE THIS TEENAGE GIRL WANTED TO BE. IDA'S PARENTS were missionaries, but soon she would be old enough to choose her future for herself. She would escape India and return to the States forever.

One night, three men came knocking at her father's door. They knew he was a doctor. "Can you help our wives?" they asked.

The visitors explained that the women were in labor and having a difficult time. The doctor ran for his bag but the men stopped him. They explained that he couldn't come. It would not be right in their culture for a man to have this kind of contact with a woman. There was no one else, and so the men left.

Ida's heart was shot through with pangs of grief. These women had endured nine months of pregnancy, yet they would probably never hold their newborns in their arms. She tried in vain to sleep.

I could not sleep that night—it was too terrible. Within the very touch of my hand were three young girls dying because there was no woman to help them. I spent much of the night in anguish and prayer. I did not want to spend my life in India. My friends were begging me to return to the joyous opportunities of a young girl in America. I went to bed in the early morning after praying for much guidance. I think that was the first time I ever met God face to face, and all that time it seemed He was calling me into this work. Early in the morning I heard the "tom tom" beating in the village and it struck terror in my heart, for it was a death message.[1]

That morning, Ida told her parents she was going home to the States—not to escape India, but to study medicine and then return to help the women of India.

That's how passion is born: God calls you and says, "Look. This is a need." You see the need, you know you can fill the need—and deep in your heart you know your life will never be the same. However, finding your passionate call is not responding to every need. God selects specific people to meet specific needs.

Ida left for her medical studies in 1895. And in a few short years, Dr. Ida Scudder returned with a medical degree and a thousand-dollar check to begin her work among the women of India. Soon other women followed her to help with the cause.

Passion Planted

The seed of passion is planted in our lives by God. Passion is not something we have to go in search of. We need to search for God. When we seek to be intimately connected with him, he will use the desires of our heart, the circumstances of our life, and his confirming Word to solidify and reveal the passion.

Passion is something you can't walk away from, because it is a part of you. I believe God places a calling on each of our lives. In the Bible, parents were sometimes told by God that their children were to accomplish a special work. The parents of John the Baptist were told, "Many of the people of Israel will he bring back to the Lord their God." And "[he will] make ready a people prepared for the Lord" (Lk 1:16-17).

Jeremiah was told by the Lord, "Before I formed you in the womb I knew you, before you were born I set you apart; I appointed you as a prophet to the nations" (Jer 1:4-5).

Passion is a gift from God to empower you. Passion is pure motivation sent through pure means to accomplish pure results that will glorify God and meet the needs of people. The method of an impassioned heart may change or adapt over time, but the passion remains constant.

For example, you may be passionate about caring for the needy, the hurting. That passion may lead you into nursing, administrating a nonprofit organization, volunteering in a service organization, launching a ministry in your local church, or creating a business that fills a niche for the needy. Same passion, different methods.

Pure Motivation
As a college freshman I was confidently going nowhere. I had dreams and desires, but my rose-colored glasses kept me from seeing the reality of my own personal ghetto. From the outside it appeared I had all I needed—a scholarship, grades, friends, a boyfriend—but inside I was struggling with huge issues. Why am I here? What difference can I make? I had been racking up awards trying to validate myself, and I had a hidden fear that I wouldn't be able to keep hauling in those awards. How many would be enough to make me feel accepted and loved? In order to gain acceptance, I felt pressure to give my heart and my sexuality away. I didn't want to. And I didn't want to live on this treadmill of acquisitions anymore either. That's when a friend invited me to a Bible study. Appropriately, that friend's name was Grace!

There I learned about the God I had met as a small girl of eight. I learned about his unconditional love and the plan he had for me that would give me a future and a hope. In the course of a year, I was a new person. I felt free to choose the best God had for me. I felt free to excel at whatever God placed in front of me and to not worry about the rest. And I was no longer driven by fear. My high-school sweetheart and I parted as friends. I started to gain a clearer picture of who I was and what the future might hold.

Pure Means

A few months later, at a leadership conference for college students, a speaker challenged us to ask God what his plans were for our lives. I found a quiet spot and began running my options by God: A congress-woman, Lord? A public relations executive? A TV anchorwoman? A teacher?

Silence.

Then God reminded me of a prayer I had prayed as a nine-year-old girl. The prayer went like this: "God, if you can arrange it, I'd really like to marry a pastor. I like the families of the pastors and missionaries I've met. And I want to tell people how they can have you for a best friend, just like you and me, God. Okay? But whether I marry a pastor or not, I want to serve you."

I told God that I agreed with the prayer I had prayed as a young girl and I would go wherever he wanted. I made a commitment that night to investigate how I might use my gifts and talents in a full-time Christian career. I knew it might still be his will that I write, teach or serve in the secular arena, but I had to be open to the option of being in ministry as a career.

In my own life, a passion for a ministry of encouraging women to become all that they were created to be formed slowly over the course of several years. God would place a young woman before me. I would disciple her. He would bring another. I would disciple her. Then one day, while I was sharing an evangelistic booklet with a student on campus, in the presence of another student whom I was discipling, a third young woman came running up to us screaming. She told the non-Christian student, "Listen to her. Listen to her. She knows what she's talking about!"

I recognized this enthusiastic woman as my next-door neighbor from the dorms a few years earlier.

"I lived in the dorms with Pam. I was in a Bible study with her—well, that is, when I came—and she told me all this stuff about God. I didn't listen then, but last year I realized Jesus was the answer I'd been looking for. My life is totally different. I'm happy for the first time in my life. It works!"

Pure Results

It works! It works! Those words rang in my head. I kept discipling and sharing Christ. A few years later, the thank-you notes began arriving in the mail. I was working on completing my education. I had continued to disciple during those years. Now I had to decide what I wanted to do with my future. I took the afternoon, closed myself away in an office and prayed. Then the Holy Spirit began to remind me of my own life.

I realized afresh that God had made a radical difference in my life. The Holy Spirit did an it's-a-wonderful-life review for me. He brought to mind girls and women one right after another who had been encouraged through my ministry: *You were my tool to get this one into ministry and married to a godly man. You were my tool to show this one that she had an artistic gift that had to be shared. You were my tool to train this one in ministry, and she's gone on to do great things for me. You were my tool to get this girl off welfare and out of an abusive relationship. This one is off drugs. This one is alive and not suicidal. This marriage is saved. This one finished college. This one went into missions . . .*

I sat in tears, humbled by the fact that God had used me. I realized I was propelled by a passion deep in my heart. I did a quick review of the women leaders I greatly respect: writers, speakers, parachurch staff women, teachers, professors, directors of women's ministries. I noticed they all had one thing in common—they had carried the gospel to their generation. In this race for the hearts and minds of women, the baton would have to pass from generation to generation. Was I willing to carry it to *my* generation?

Yes, Lord.

Fear of Passion

Passion is intense. You may be reluctant to be impassioned—overwhelmed at the challenge of letting yourself answer the call of God. You may fear the unknown. You may fear the responsibility of carrying the burden. Or you may fear burnout from caring too much. You may also feel inadequate or unprepared to carry the passion.

My biggest struggle with my own passion is that at times it feels too big. Intense emotions are carried in my heart. In fact, I feel as if I carry the world like a heart-shaped locket around my neck. I see a world of injustice, and my heart swells with passion. How can I become numb to the 23 million refugees, three-quarters of them women and children, fleeing war, rape, violence and hunger? How can I stand idly by when in India and China alone there are 77 million fewer women than there should be because of sex-selection abortions?

An ad in India said it is better to spend $38 now on an abortion than $3800 later on a dowry. And the same dowry system, once a celebration showering money and gifts on a new couple, has grown into a blackmail system where a prospective husband demands a dowry or threatens not to marry. Then after the marriage, the demands keep coming. If the demands are not met, the bride may be set on fire by her new husband, who often claims that she died in a kitchen accident. In India alone the official count was 4,835 bride burnings in 1990.

Each year about a million girls worldwide suffer female circumcision, or genital mutilation. Some die; some become infertile. In developing countries, two girls out of five get no education, even though it has been shown that a mother's educational level is the key factor in lowering child mortality rates. Seven years of education for a woman will lower infant mortality by 75 percent.

Indoor cooking was identified in a 1992 World Development report as one of four major environmental health hazards. It is estimated that 700 million women and children worldwide are breathing air that is equivalent to smoking three to five packs of cigarettes a day. Worldwide, women grow half the food, but receive only 10 percent of the world's income and own only 1 percent of the world's property.[2]

The white picket fences of the United States are by no means stopping the injustices. Domestic problems include battered women, undereducated women, substance abuse, depression, suicide and much more! Since 1960 there has been a 560 percent increase in violent crime and a 400 percent increase in out-of-wedlock births. The divorce rate quadrupled while the number of children living in single parent homes tripled. Teen suicide rose 200 percent, and SAT scores plummeted.[3]

In today's headlines we read of women who are in desperate need of help, evidenced by their horrendous actions. One mother drowned her two preschool boys in a lake, then faked their kidnapping, and a nation searched for weeks while the two tiny bodies lay in their watery grave. Another mother, who held a master's degree in special education and worked as a teacher and guidance counselor, allowed her AIDS-infected new husband to have intercourse with her seven-year-old daughter during the wedding reception!

Add to that the number of women who live far below their potential just because someone along the way told them that they were stupid, ugly or untalented. The clincher for me is that two-thirds of all people in the U.S. haven't understood God in a way they can respond to.[4]

Feeling overwhelmed? I am. It's easy to want to pull the cozy coverlet over your head and stay in bed.

Passion in the Real World

One afternoon I was driving to meet my husband for dinner. My little boys were in the back seat of my car. It was a chilly afternoon, and the overcast clouds made all of life seem gray. I drove down a residential street, near an elementary school. On my left, I saw a young man and woman arguing. I watched the couple carefully as I approached. There was fear in her face. The man began to push the girl, then to hit her. The street was full of cars, but no one was stopping.

She could be battered! She could be raped! He has to be stopped! My heart was screaming to my head. I signaled and pulled over next to the car into which the man was now trying to force the woman. I slammed on my brakes, rolled down my window and yelled, "Leave her alone—right now! I'm going to phone the police, so you'd better let her go and get out of here!" The young woman broke free and raced toward a nearby home.

By this time I had caused a traffic jam, so I quickly pulled back onto the road and turned the corner. Another driver pulled to the side of the road and waved to me. "Is she okay?" she asked. Then she called the police on her car phone.

Just then another car pulled up behind us. I quickly checked to see if the angry man was now coming after me. This was the same block where a gang shooting had occurred just a few weeks before, and the potential consequences of my actions were dawning on me. I sighed with relief when I saw it was another woman. She pulled up next to me and lowered her window.

"Thought I'd let you know that girl got into the house, and her boyfriend—or whatever—sped away in his car."

"Thanks," I said.

"You bet. I saw it too, but I didn't know what to do," the unknown woman confessed.

"I know—I just prayed and reacted!" I said, swallowing my pounding heart that seemed to be beating its way up my throat. The woman with the car phone came back and said the police had just received a 911 call from the house, were on their way and didn't need us.

I started to drive. My three-year-old said, "Mom, do you think that man has a gun and will come shoot us?" Then I started to cry.

God, he could have shot us. He could have pulled out a gun and in anger shot at me and hit one of my babies instead! But God, I felt that my actions were from your heart. If that had been my daughter, I would have wanted someone to do what I did. This burden is so heavy, God. If I see injustice, I just act. Guard my family. Give me wisdom. Don't take away the passion—just temper it with your protection.

Still shaking, I drove toward the restaurant where we were to meet Bill. My mind wandered back to a news story I had heard when I was a young woman. Kitty Genovese had been brutally attacked as she returned to her apartment. For thirty minutes she screamed and cried as her life was beaten out of her. She cried for help but none came. The next day, as the police were investigating the murder, they found thirty-eight people who had witnessed the attack from their apartment windows. Not one even picked up the phone to call for assistance. Not one.[5]

God, I can't walk away. I can't ignore the hurt in this world. I can't stay silent. I'm asking you to bridle this passion when it needs to bridled and unleash it with all its fury when it needs to be unleashed. This is your heart planted in me, so please take care of your heart.

Passion Protected

She was young and beautiful. Heads turned when she entered a room. She was married to a powerful, rich man, and life seemed perfect. Perfect except for a secret that she kept hidden from everyone, including her husband. Only her family knew who she really was.

Then one day she heard of a plot that would harm her family, her culture and her future. The leader of a radical extremist group had gained the confidence of her husband and arranged for the wholesale slaughter of her entire people. She was safe—the secret of her ethnic identity hadn't gotten out—but others were in danger. Her perfect life was crumbling before her eyes. What should she do?

She received a stealth visit from her uncle. After he left, his words rang in her heart. "Who knows, maybe you have come to this position for such a time as this." She promised her uncle that she would go to her husband on behalf of her people. Her secret would be out. Her life would be on the line. With all the courage she could find, she asked those closest to her to pray, saying, "If I perish, I perish" (Esther 4:16 NASB).

But Esther didn't perish. She and her people were saved. Esther was transformed from a timid trembler to a passionate princess by God's passion planted within her. God takes care of his impassioned people. He lets me know when to act and when to be still. He lets me know when and how far to step in. I'm not so afraid, because God is carrying the burden for the passion he placed within me.

Passion on Hold

It seems strange when it happens, but God will sometimes fill your heart with passion and then make you wait! At times, his purpose for your life is best accomplished when he puts your passion on hold.

God didn't allow us to enter full-time Christian work right away. We had a lot of schooling to take care of. I worked and put Bill through an undergraduate program while we simultaneously volunteered in youth ministry. We were looking forward to graduation and then going right into a youth ministry position. But a colleague in ministry suggested that, since we wanted a lifelong professional ministry, seminary training would be a wise investment. My heart was a mixture of humble obedience and broken dreams. I cried all night in God's waiting room. I didn't know how to put my passion on hold. More schooling meant more waiting, and I was tired of waiting.

Because what seemed to be God's leading was so hard for us to accept, we counseled with the associate pastor of our church. This gracious man pointed out to us that God, having placed his calling in us, was holding us back so our passion would build, much as a glowing ember can grow into a blazing fire. He explained that God was ensuring that our passion would be strong enough to carry us through even the toughest of times. Sitting in God's waiting room transformed our passion into a sacrificial attitude of *whatever it takes, Lord.*

Passion Unfurled

Passion is sometimes planted by pain. Elizabeth Mittelstaedt loves to encourage others. Little did she realize that a routine dental procedure in Germany would be the beginning of a long process of God's planting passion in her heart.

Something went terribly wrong at the dentist's. For the next ten years, she went from professional to professional for help in alleviating her unbearable, ongoing pain. Finally, one doctor presented her with a tough reality: "There's nothing more that can be done to repair the damage or relieve your pain. You'll have to live with it."

How could she live with this pain? Despairing, Elizabeth went for a walk one morning near her home in Frankfurt, Germany. As she crossed a small bridge, the frustration of her life overwhelmed her. She could not fathom how she could live with such intense pain. She felt useless to help anyone else when her daily routine was such a chore. She was drained of hope. She felt an intense urge to jump off the bridge and end all the pain.

At that moment, the story of Satan tempting Jesus came into her head, and Elizabeth said to herself, *No, I'm not going to jump. I am going to trust God.* As she looked out over the skyline, God spoke to her heart. She was captivated by the thought that women all across Europe were experiencing all kinds of pain. She was enveloped by the sense that there was a sisterhood of women intimately connected by their suffering. She no longer felt so alone in her pain.

That morning a vision for a women's magazine was born. This was her opportunity to help European women find the strength to go on and rebuild their lives. Women across Europe had lived under communist oppression, poverty, poor health care and spiritual darkness. Her passion gave birth to *Lydia*, a magazine that offers hope to women through practical information, personal inspiration and spiritual direction.[6]

The passion we are talking about is not just a feeling. Feelings can be acted upon if it is convenient. Passion *must* be acted on! Passion's roots run deep and are wrapped around deep-rooted beliefs. Those convictions are the difference between a feeling that goes up in flames quickly and an eternal fiery bush that burns yet is not consumed. Convictions are the staying power for passion. How do you discover what those convictions are?

The best way to discover what you are truly passionate about is to ask yourself a few key questions. What truths would I die for? What principles would I go to jail to protect? What people would I place my neck on the chopping block for? And why would I do it?

Passion to Die For

Many women could sail through their entire lives never faced with a life-and-death decision. We in the Western world can easily give lip service to various causes or principles. We become lax in our faith. We may *hope* that if it came right down to it we would say, "I would rather die than break my faith."[7] Those were the words Ann Askew actually spoke to the Lord Chancellor in the tumult of the Reformation. She was one of many brave women burned at the stake for their Christian beliefs.

When A. Wetherell Johnson was a young missionary in China, she led a girl to faith in Christ. The young woman began to attend a Bible-study group, and one morning she stopped by to see Miss Johnson. "After yesterday afternoon, I decided I would never again worship idols."

It was the custom in this woman's home, as in most homes in China, to bow before the house idol each morning before leaving for school or work. She was the youngest of twelve children, and when it was finally her turn, she stood up straight and said, "I worship Jesus and I cannot bow down to the idol."

Her mother and father tried to talk her into it. When she would not give in, her father took her out and beat her unmercifully all over her body with rods. She still refused to worship the idol.

When she recounted the story to Miss Johnson, Miss Johnson began to weep. But the young woman said, "Don't cry, Teacher. The Lord was with me just as he was with the three Israelites in the fire, and he has taken the sting away."[8]

Over the centuries, many courageous women have died for their faith. One of the first recorded women martyrs was Perpetua. Her writings and the accounts of eyewitnesses record the events of the early third century. Perpetua was born to a wealthy family, and she had a slave about her same age, Felicitas. These two young mothers had come to faith in Christ and refused to renounce their faith in him.

They were stripped and thrown into an arena with a mad cow. Even the bloodthirsty crowds at the coliseum were aghast at the sight of a new mother, breasts dripping with milk, thrown naked into such a pit. So the two were recalled, given loosely fitting gowns and sent back out. Perpetua was hit first and knocked to the ground. She sat up and, seeing that her gown had been torn, fumbled with the fabric to maintain her modesty. She stopped to clip back her hair because she thought it not proper that a martyr be disheveled. She stood to her feet. She saw Felicitas, bruised and broken, and ran to help her. Becoming impatient, the crowd demanded that the two women be brought out into the open and die by the sword. Perpetua and Felicitas voluntarily moved out to the center of the arena.

The gladiators silently sliced into the martyrs. Perpetua groaned as the sword plunged into her side. She lifted her head, took the trembling hand of the gladiator and pointed to her throat.[9]

Perpetua chose to die for the One who had died for her.

I want to think I would be brave like Perpetua and Felicitas. But what does it mean to die for the faith? One day, in a quiet time with God, I took my church's doctrinal statement and the doctrinal statements of several Christian organizations and seminaries. I wanted to know what truths I'd die for. I reasoned that if I knew what I would die for, I would know what to live for. Here are some basic tenets I listed:

The inerrancy of Scripture. My personal relationship with Jesus Christ is based upon truth: the Bible. Therefore, if the Bible is the basis for my relationship, I must be ready to defend it. God's Word is life. My heart would soon dry up without the precious nourishment from God's Word, so I knew this was the first issue to live for—or die for.

The character of God. God is triune. He is the all-knowing, all-loving Creator and Sustainer of life. He is wholly good, righteous and unchanging. He is all-powerful and always faithful. God lacks nothing. He is utterly dependable

The deity of Christ. If Christ was not the eternal, incarnate God who died for the sins of human beings, then his sacrifice would not be eternal and complete. It would be limited, and my faith would be in vain. Jesus *is* God, and his sacrifice *is* complete.

The Holy Spirit is God. Jesus said another of the same kind would come to comfort, lead and guide us. God resides in me to live through me.

I am sinful. My personal sinfulness separates me from the holy God. I am utterly imperfect; therefore, I need a mediator to reconnect my relationship. Christ is that mediator. Salvation is impossible through any other means.

The church. The church universal is God's method for reaching the world with his love. No, I won't die for a building, but I will die for the right to assemble, worship and proclaim the truth.

I also read through the Constitution, the Bill of Rights and Declaration of Independence. I would go to court for most of the words in those

documents, but I knew I'd die for only a few of their tenets. The right
to govern ourselves in a democracy is important to me. I'd also spend
the rest of my life in a jail cell for the First Amendment, guaranteeing
freedom of religion and freedom of speech. For people to continue
coming to Christ, the pen and the voice cannot be silenced. If need be,
I'd join my courageous sisters and brothers who spent years in
concentration camps, behind communist walls or in the cells of hostile
religious countries for the right to tell of Jesus.

I would also go to jail, if necessary, for my right to bear and raise
my own children, my right to be married, my right to vote, my right to
live out my Christian convictions. What good is a faith if you can't live
it out?

Then I asked myself *who* I would be willing to die for. My husband,
my children, friends, relatives . . . those I was discipling . . . the innocent
and oppressed . . . the list grew.

And then I remembered, "Rarely will anyone die for a righteous
person—though perhaps for a good person someone might actually
dare to die. But God proves his own love for us in that while we still
were sinners Christ died for us" (Rom 5:7-8 NRSV). Would I die for the
unrighteous, the unholy, my enemies? My answer: *Yes, Lord. I am willing
to risk my life if you give me the wisdom to know when to stand up for
the oppressed and when to speak up to the oppressor.*

Passion Purified

In *A Man for All Seasons,* Sir Thomas More, faced with execution, is
asked by the king and his court to recant his views of the king's divorce
and remarriage. His family also comes and asks him to change his views.
More replies, "When a man takes an oath . . . he's holding his own self
in his hands. Like water. And if he opens his fingers, then he needn't
hope to find himself again."[10] I believe that to deny my convictions is
to deny myself. Rejecting the passion we have been given will make
life meaningless.

What so beats in your heart that if it were to vanish, you would no longer be you? Like Jeremiah, you can discover your passion. He said, "But if I say, 'I will not mention him or speak any more in his name,' his word is in my heart like a fire, a fire shut up in my bones. I am weary of holding it in; indeed, I cannot" (Jer 20:9). Jeremiah was called to be a prophet. He was a proclaimer of God's truth. Even if the people didn't respond—and they didn't—he still proclaimed. When he got tired of the poor results and wanted to quit, he still proclaimed. Even his body would react if he didn't proclaim, because he was born to be a proclaimer! What were you born to be?

You can discover the passion that God designed *uniquely for you*. What is on your mind as you go to sleep at night and then first thing in the morning? When you sit for those rare quiet moments and daydream, where do your thoughts take you? What movies bring you to tears? What injustices make your blood boil? When you read God's Word, are there common themes in the verses you mark? What breaks your heart?

Florence Nightingale was a selfless angel of mercy during the Crimean War and in the halls of London hospitals. In her journal she penned her passion for nursing: "O God, Thou puttest into my heart this great desire to devote myself to the sick and sorrowful. I offer it to Thee."[11]

Florence fought for sanitation, good food and accurate records. In 1860 she founded the first school of modern nursing at St. Thomas's Hospital in London. It was not acceptable at that time for a woman to work so closely with the ill, but her passion propelled her past the stereotypes.

Once, after working and nursing the ill among peasant women, she wrote: "Now I know what it is to live and to love life. . . . I wish for no other earth, no other world than this."[12]

Have you discovered what it means "to live and to love life"? God promises to lift us up to our high place. You have the opportunity to say with the prophet Habakkuk, "The Lord GOD is my strength, and

He has made my feet like hinds' feet, and makes me walk on my high places" (Hab 3:19 NASB). Passion will carry you to *your* high place. It is when you are there, in the place of your passion, that you can say, "I know who I was born to be." Passion—it works!

Living It Out

When you find that which breaks the heart that Christ placed in you, then you will find your passion. Write three sentences that capture times when you were moved to tears, decided on some action or resolved to reach out.

Now interview one family member and two close friends. Ask them what topics they notice you bringing up most often. Are there any similarities between the list you made and what the interviews reveal?

Finally, take your lists to the Lord. Also take a statement of faith from your church or a Christian organization. Ask God to show you what you are to live for. Commit the passion of your heart to God in prayer.

Chapter 2

A Woman
of Influence
Is an Individual

I LOVE HATS. ONE OF THE WALLS IN MY BEDROOM HOLDS SEVERAL THAT I'VE picked up at sales over the years. Hats finish off an outfit. Recently a friend sent me an article about people who wear hats. A hat expert was quoted as saying that the only thing that doesn't go well with a hat is timidity. "You have to be more self-assured to wear a hat. . . . The moment you don't care what people think is the moment you've arrived."[1] Women often comment to me, "Oh, I love your hats. I'd like to wear hats, but I don't look good in them." My usual reply is, "You just haven't found the right hat! Wearing a hat is an attitude you put on."

Carol Navratil, a courageous woman facing cancer, was given a "hat shower" by friends at a cancer rebound group. The press came and interviewed her. They asked how she had handled the transition from having hair to wearing hats. Her answer was her attitude. Donning a hat, she said, "Walk like it's supposed to be there."[2]

Being a woman of influence is a matter of finding the right hat. "For we are God's workmanship, created in Christ Jesus to do good works, which God prepared in advance for us to do" (Eph 2:10). He has promised to equip us for every good work; we just have to put on the hat!

Are We Really So Different?

So when we put on the leadership hat, how do we lead? Studies differ on the way men and women approach leadership. Sally Helgesen kept a diary that followed the lives of successful female executives and entrepreneurs. She found that women managers had many of the same characteristics as their male counterparts but that they also had a few distinctive character traits.[3]

She found that women managers

1. worked at a steady pace, as men did, but women guarded short "down times" to catch their breath and clear their mind throughout the day.

2. made a deliberate attempt to be accessible. One study showed that women managers were twice as accessible as their male counterparts.[4]

3. integrated family and work. Men tended to compartmentalize their lives while women blended them. It may be natural for a woman manager to make out her grocery list or talk to her children on the phone in the five minutes between meetings. However, men *and* women who carried a role conflict, being torn between family and work responsibilities, both wanted company policies that were more family-friendly, such as job sharing, flex time and child care.[5]

4. preferred live personal contacts. Just like the male managers, females prefer conversations and delegation to be as personal as possible: they like face-to-face contact better than phone, memo or fax.

5. maintained a complex network of relationships outside the

organization. Male managers spent equivalent time in outside contacts, but the women's networks were broader, often including volunteer organizations, ministry and personal interests that didn't seem as connected to the job.

6. focused on the ecology of leadership. They kept the long term in focus, while some male counterparts often felt buried in the "today."

7. saw their own identity as complex. A woman is not her career. Their careers were just one element of who women saw themselves to be.

8. scheduled time to share information. Women in leadership held relationships in high value. Women tended to see interruptions by people as an opportunity to share and build the relationship, not an interruption of a task.

However, these differences are very slight and narrowing. Women are slightly better at verbal skills, reading nonverbal clues, maintaining high energy and holding their own inner work standard. Men are slightly better at spatial tasks, attentiveness to power structures, task-oriented behaviors, and, most important, men had a better ability to see themselves as leaders.[6]

These differences can lead to complementary leadership styles, especially as women grow in self-confidence. When a woman has interacted with a group for an extended period and her leadership style is defined, others then see her competence. As she absorbs their responses to her, she then sees herself as a leader—and so does the group.[7]

We are all unique. God plants within each of us desires, dreams, talents and skills to be used for his glory. Each of us has our own "hat" of responsibility to wear, and each is a different kind of leader—we can influence the world around us uniquely.

On the next few pages you will find a leadership style test. I created this test after studying the roles of women in the Bible. It amazed me that women so different from each other could all be used by God in dramatic ways. This test can help you learn more about how God can use you as a woman of influence.

Leadership Style Test

Place the number that best describes you in front of each statement. Give the sentence 3 points if it is *very true* about you, 2 points if it is *sometimes true* and 1 point if it is *rarely true*. If you aren't sure, then ask yourself, "Do I do this because I know it's right, or do I love doing it because it's who I am?" If it is out of obligation, give the statement a lower number. Remember, you are trying to discern the leadership style that you'll best function in.

Leadership Style #1

___I am drawn to detail work.

___I notice those who need help (ill, hurting and so on), and I don't run away from needy people.

___I like to create quietly.

___I enjoy meeting the physical needs of others (food, water, medical care and so on).

___I like having company in my home. I see myself as hospitable.

___I want my material possessions to be used to help others, so I don't mind lending them out.

___I like to nurture or encourage one-on-one, or even silently by doing nice things.

___My friends see me as a mother at heart.

___I don't mind serving. In fact, I don't like the spotlight, so I avoid drawing attention to something I've done.

___Others compliment me on my ability to sacrifice.

___Total

Leadership Style #2

___I feel prayer accomplishes more than busywork.

___I look forward to private worship and enjoy leading others in worship.

___When someone asks me to pray, I make it a priority to remember to do it.

___I like to use my talents as a way to worship God rather than just to meet people's needs.

___I like to keep track of answers to prayer or prayer requests.

___I understand the need for spiritual warfare, and I like to equip others in this area.

___I like to be part of helping the tough-case people, such as drug addicts, gangs or the sexually deviant.

___I don't enjoy the spotlight or crowds.

___Others thank me for "being there" for them in tough times.

___I like to counsel others when they are having problems.

___Total

Leadership Style #3

___Time gets away from me when I study the Bible. I enjoy long blocks of study time.

___I like to prepare lesson plans. I can pick the main points out of what I read or hear.

___I like to teach a consistent group of people.

___I like to disciple younger believers.

___I look for opportunities to share with others what I know, so they can know it too.

___I prefer having a few close friends rather than many acquaintances.

___I like to see pupils succeed, even if they pass me on the professional ladder.

___I like to help clarify people's thinking.

___Others thank me for teaching them how to do things.

___I would rather manage people than products.

___Total

Leadership Style #4

___I like to speak in public.

___I like meeting new people.

___I like discussions, even if they get lively.

___Hearing opposing opinions doesn't make me any less sure of my own. I'm not afraid of taking a public stand.

___I regularly read the opinion page, listen to talk radio and watch TV news shows.

___I love magazines and books because I can use things I've learned from them in conversation.

___I like to persuade others.

___I am drawn to sales or spokesperson positions.

___I am comfortable talking about my personal religious beliefs in public.

___Others compliment my verbal skills.

___Total

Leadership Style #5

___I was a cheerleader, or I wanted to be one, when I was younger.

___Others see me as a visionary. I love to dream and plan.

___I see the potential in people and circumstances.

___I enjoy inspiring others and coaching them to their best.

___I regularly write notes of encouragement or send cards for special occasions.

___I have a long Christmas-card list.

___I am comfortable in social settings.

___I like sentimental things like poetry, tear-jerker movies and photo albums.

___I am an optimist.

___Others thank me for believing in them.

___Total

Add up your points for each leadership style. You will probably be strongest in one or two areas. If you have the same score in all areas, retake the test, asking yourself if this is really how you see yourself, or have someone who knows you well take the test as if they are answering for you. Sometimes we want to see ourselves differently from how we really are.

The goal is not to pigeonhole you but to expose you to the leader within. It is meant to expose you to a variety of leadership styles so that you can confidently create your own! God designed you to influence your world; he wants you to see how you can accomplish this task while still being yourself. The descriptions below will clarify the various leadership styles.

Leadership Style #1: The Provider

"Render service with enthusiasm, as to the Lord and not to men and women" (Eph 6:7 NRSV).

This woman leads from behind the scenes. She may be a gifted administrator. She may also have the gift of helps, mercy, hospitality or giving. The key trait of a *provider* is that she sees a need and quietly goes about the task of providing for the need. The provider hates the limelight. She won't call a press conference or rally the troops to get a need met. However, providers are strategic at networking a small group of people together to accomplish a task.

Providers have an ability to see the details. Details don't usually fall through the cracks with the provider. Providers stick to the task until it is complete, and they stick to the person until the person is stable and self-sufficient. Loyalty is the trait for which they are often rewarded. Providers lead from an open heart.

Providers seem drawn to professions where they can work quietly and consistently. It is in their faithfulness to the least of tasks that they gain their leadership platform. It is the providers who keep computer systems up and running, who staff hospitals, who run hotels, who make our food, and who keep organizations running. Providers are leaders

like Martha, who took care of the physical needs of the Savior while
he ministered. These women are behind the scenes making matzos,
but their maturity runs deep. It was Martha who said, when her brother
died, "Lord, . . . if you had been here, my brother would not have died.
But I know that even now God will give you whatever you ask" (Jn
11:21-22).

The first church of Acts wouldn't have gotten off the ground without
the hostesses of the house churches. The temple wouldn't have run
without women like Anna, who served night and day making preparations. And the personal touch would have been missing from the
budding church without women like Tabitha, Phoebe and Lydia, who
moved about quietly in their communities, providing for the needs of
the less fortunate.

Providers sometimes are given a great ability to earn money and use
it generously. They often see all their possessions as gifts from God
and readily share their material goods to help others. One provider
friend of mine has a special calling to encourage women in ministry.
She was raised in a ministry home, so she knows firsthand the unique
stresses and pressures. She uses her gift of hospitality and helps to
refresh those on the front lines.

A mother who is a provider always has extra snacks for the hordes
of children who play at her house. The only downfall of a provider is
that she is so good at sacrificing for the need that she may judge others
by their ability to sacrifice. Children raised with a mother who parades
her sacrifices can become bitter and guilty. But a mother who is truly
sacrificial won't make herself a martyr, because she sees her sacrifice
as just meeting the need of the moment.

Providers are moved to action by their compassion. One mother of
ten children was asked which was her favorite child. Her answer, "The
one who, at the moment, needs me the most."

Susannah Wesley had the heart of a provider. She studied Greek,
Latin, French, logic and metaphysics—and she loved the Bible. She

used her knowledge as she singlehandedly home-schooled her ten children. (She bore nineteen! But only ten survived past infancy.) She also began a Bible study in her living room; it grew to a group of over two hundred. Her mothering style was very deliberate. She taught her children from 9 a.m. till noon and listened to their recitations of verses from 2 to 5 p.m. daily. The discipline and self-control learned at their mother's knee launched two of her sons, Charles and John, into a dynamic work for God as they founded the Methodist movement.[8]

Whether you are single or married, a mom or a grandmother, a part of you really cares that things are done right. You want life to run smoothly and efficiently, and people depend on you for your ability to make that happen. Your caring thoroughness will ensure your influence.

Leadership Style #2: The Petitioner

"This kind can come out only by prayer" (Mk 9:29).

The *petitioner* is an advocate. She sees her role as one of a representative. She may exercise her gifts and represent the needs of others to God through prayer. She may also be drawn into the field of law or social work. A petitioner can also be the one who takes on the tough ministries to gangs, inmates, addicts and others who are spiritually bound up by sin or circumstance. The petitioner has an admirable quality of outward fearlessness because she has an inward surety from God. There are no "tough neighborhoods" to a petitioner. She understands and communicates the need for spiritual warfare as a way to solve problems. She may be drawn to counseling because of her keen insight. People in need have a way of landing on her doorstep.

Deborah was a petitioner. God called Deborah to be a judge in a time in Israel's history when people were "doing that which was right in their own eyes." She was spiritually in tune, and people knew it. She would sit under a tree and people would come from all around to have her judge their cases. But Deborah didn't just sit under the tree; she also got up and got involved. Barak, the general of the Israelite army, asked Deborah to go into battle with him—so Deborah went! And Israel won.

Mothers with these traits often see their children's friends come to them for advice. These mothers start prayer groups, organize a "neighborhood watch" and float petitions. Mothers with this leadership style pray first and lecture little. One of my friends with this gift was asked by my son to pray for his "owie." When I asked him why he asked her instead of me, he said, "Mom, I know you can pray for me, but she prays all the time. I thought it would work quicker!"

Petitioner moms can be accused of overspiritualizing problems. One of my boys gets a little unruly if he is tired or hungry. Once a petitioner friend was amazed to see how quickly his negative mood became positive after he ate a sandwich. She confided to me that she had been praying for him because she thought he had a rebellious bent. I told her to keep praying because we all have a rebellious bent!

Elizabeth Dole has served under six presidents. In 1991 she became the first woman to serve as president of the Red Cross since Clara Barton. She's a bulldog fighting for good causes. Elizabeth grew into her leadership style under the examples of her grandmother and mother. Her grandmother lost a son when he was killed by a drunk driver. Every cent from the insurance policy went to build a mission hospital overseas. Her most vivid memory of her mother is of her kneeling in prayer.

Elizabeth looks for ways to give back to the community and make a difference. She loves giving reverse birthday parties, where guests bring donations for charity. Her first was a party at Sarah's Circle, a church-sponsored organization that houses the homeless in Washington, D.C. "We can't take all God gives us, then do nothing for those less fortunate. The questions I'll want to ask myself when I'm ninety years old and looking back over my life are not, How much money did I make? and How many titles, awards, or honors did I receive? But rather, What did I stand for? Did I make a positive difference for others?"[9]

Leadership Style #3: The Preparer

"All Scripture is God-breathed and is useful for teaching, rebuking, correcting and training in righteousness" (2 Tim 3:16).

The woman who leads by preparing has the heart of a teacher. The minute she gains a skill, she wants to give it away by training someone else. She may be very accomplished in her field, but her real delight is training and equipping others. A *preparer* never minds when her pupils pass her on the professional ladder. In fact, she expects it and rejoices in it.

The preparer gets lost in studying. This woman loves the library, books, research, outlining, lesson prep, and often loses track of time when she is immersed in study or prep work.

The preparer loves to teach the same consistent group of students for a specific length of time, because growth in her students is her greatest reward. She doesn't mind speaking, but she does it for the purpose of equipping others with necessary skills, rather than teaching just because she can't keep quiet! Her method is her message. She wants others to have the "how-to's" of life. Mentoring and discipleship are natural for preparers.

Priscilla had the heart of a preparer. She, with her husband, took Apollos aside to tutor him in theology because he hadn't received a complete education (see Acts 18:24-28). She better equipped Apollos for his preaching ministry.

Moms that are preparers have children who do household chores well at an early age. Preparers have the patience to teach and the conviction that it is important. Preparers may love leading groups of children in learning crafts or cooking. Kids love the homes of preparers, because they come away feeling smarter.

However, preparer moms should also watch out for the "my way is the right way" mentality, because it can easily creep into their teaching. If this happens, their children and those under their influence will feel defeated.

A. Wetherell Johnson, the founder of Bible Study Fellowship, had the heart of a preparer. Her method of small-group discussion, accompanied by a lecture, take-home study notes and a lesson, has become a model for ministries throughout the world. Early in her ministry, she was asked to speak to a group of young people. She didn't want to just give her testimony, so she decided to speak on a text. "I thought it would be easy," she writes, "but I finished with embarrassment in less than five minutes, recognizing too late that speaking for God needed careful preparation."[10] She went back and began preparing! And it is for her preparation skills that she is best known.

Leadership Style #4: The Proclaimer
"I have not hesitated to proclaim to you the whole will of God" (Acts 20:27).

This woman *loves* to talk! She is comfortable meeting new people, and she has strong verbal skills. She loves to debate, negotiate, moderate and emcee events. She always has a story to tell. The *proclaimer* leads by being the spokesperson. She is not afraid to speak in public, and she's not afraid to take a public stand for her beliefs. She is tenacious when criticized and believes that the bad speech of others should be answered with more speech. She doesn't want her critics silenced, because she longs to persuade them to join her side.

The proclaimer gravitates to careers where she can earn a living by talking. She may be a salesperson, a service representative, a spokesperson, actor, talk-show host or media personality. Often, you'll find proclaimers in politics, serving as lobbyists or public relations specialists. In volunteer organizations, the proclaimer is usually the one with the most contact with the public.

Beverly LaHaye has the heart of a proclaimer. During the seventies, she felt most women's opinions were not being addressed. She gathered a group of women together in 1979 and formed Concerned Women for America. Today this group has exploded to over 600,000 members, much larger than the more media-publicized National Organization of Women.

Moms who are proclaimers are fun at the dinner table and bedtime, because they have great stories to tell. Their children often form opinions about serious issues at an early age. The children of proclaimers will always know the political affiliation of the proclaimer. Proclaimer parents have to watch out for lecturing when they should be listening.

Once, when I was at a gathering of my extended family, I was rattling on about some serious, world-changing issue when my brother reached under the sofa and acted as if he was pulling out a drawer. Thinking that was an odd gesture, I asked, "What are you doing?" He pointed at the imaginary item and said, "It's a soapbox, Pam. Looks like you left yours at home."

Huldah was a proclaimer who was summoned by King Josiah. Josiah found a scroll and wanted to know if it was of God. Huldah was probably a teacher, perhaps one who taught women from her home near the temple. Huldah confirmed that the scroll was of God. She also gave Josiah an encouraging prophecy regarding his future—and a harsh prophecy for rebellious Israel's future. Because of Huldah's brave proclamation, Josiah ordered the reading of the scroll before all of Israel. It is interesting that in the brief description of Huldah's proclamation, "This is what the LORD says" is recorded four times. Huldah obviously knew she was just a vessel, simply a voice for God (2 Kings 22:14-20; 2 Chron 34:22-28).

Sometimes people think proclaimers were born with a silver microphone in their hands, but often God raises proclaimers out of obscurity. Amanda Smith was a scrubwoman born into slavery. She married twice. Her first husband abandoned her, and the second died. As a Negro widow in the post-Civil War era, her options for employment were slim.

Amanda had always loved God and been faithful to the church. Soon after her second husband's death, she felt a distinct call to preach. This was a very unlikely career decision. She traveled throughout the North and South, over to England and then to India. Because of her gender, Amanda was sometimes thought of as an agitator for the ordination of women or women's voting rights. She replied, "The thought of ordination had never once entered my mind, for I had received my ordination from Him who said, 'Ye have not chosen Me but I have chosen you, and ordained you, that you might go and bring forth fruit.' "[11] Amanda's passion was to proclaim as an obedient servant.

Leadership Style #5: The Praiser

"Let us consider how we may spur one another on toward love and good deeds" (Heb 10:24).

The *praiser* is the woman who leads by encouragement. She cheerleads; she coaches others on her team toward success. Often this kind of leader is gifted with the ability to have great faith in God and believe him for the seemingly impossible. Others see her as a visionary, because she can picture a bright future and strategize about ways to get there. The praiser is the woman who sees the potential in everyone.

Because the praiser is so good with people, she gathers friends as some women gather flowers. Her Christmas-card list is a mile long, because staying in touch with people is of vital importance to her. She is not afraid of her emotions, and she allows herself to express emotional sentiments freely, especially if another person will be strengthened. Her greatest asset is her optimism.

Children of praisers have great self-esteem! These women are the perpetual team moms. A praiser never misses an opportunity to applaud her child. Her children's friends love to play at the praiser's home, because it's always like a party and everyone leaves feeling good. However, this same idealism can be the source of pain for the praiser and her family. Because the praiser is such an optimist, she can fall into the trap of overinflating her strengths or the strengths of her children. If they fail, it may feel like a crushing blow.

Praisers are so optimistic that some people feel intimidated. Others think that the praiser's high goals and aspirations are so lofty that to do anything less than measure up is to fail. A true praiser sets high goals because that will give God plenty of space in which to work. She sees any shortcoming as only a minor setback or a challenge that will cause further growth. Any movement at all is reason for excitement for the praiser. Her goal is just to inspire others to try.

The biggest obstacle in the way of women's success is not lack of education or lack of ability. Rather, the biggest obstacle is a lack of motivation and the inability to believe in what you think is God's will for you. When I was a young Christian, the poetry of Ann Kimmel Anderson helped form my own gift of leadership. She inspired me to "love the word *impossible!*" I think that's why women with this leadership style are found in a broad range of professions. Every team needs a cheerleader; every person needs hope.

Miriam was a praiser. Exodus 15:20-21 gives the account of God parting the Red Sea to free Israel from Egyptian bondage. Miriam, seizing the moment, grabbed a tambourine and began to dance. Thousands of women probably poured out to join in the singing and dancing. Miriam sang God's praise: "Sing to the LORD, for he is highly exalted. The horse and his rider he has hurled into the sea." Israel needed to learn to praise again. Miriam, now well over eighty, cheered them into praise.

Who Is Your Audience?

God enhances our uniqueness and focuses our talent with our leadership style. In Israel, gifted handcrafters, artists and musicians were set apart for special work for the temple. In the same way, our leadership styles dictate the way in which we use the talents God gives us. Often, the audience we are trying to reach helps us focus in on our leadership style and find the best use of our gifts.

For example, some solo recording artists have a burden to sing to reach the unchurched, while others sing to inspire the church to action. Two different audiences, two different callings, but the same talent. Try to discern who you want to lead as well as your leadership style.

Breaking the Stained-Glass Ceiling

For a woman to be free to lead, she must answer her own questions on the role of women in leadership. For centuries, the debate has raged over women's roles in leadership. Below are some theological thoughts from a few modern women leaders.

Anne Graham Lotz, daughter of renowned evangelist Billy Graham, explains her calling to teach the Word of God around the world by comparing her life to that of Mary Magdalene. Mary followed Jesus. She sat under his teaching. She followed him through his ordeal on the cross when all his disciples but John fled. She followed him as he was taken off the cross, and she helped prepare him for burial. She came, early one morning, bringing costly spices to his tomb. There Jesus revealed himself to her and told her to go and tell his disciples.

Just as Mary was commissioned, so Anne feels commissioned. "The authority is not in a position that I hold. The authority is in the Word of God and the power of the Holy Spirit that clothes it." The key is a servant's heart and an obedient attitude.

"I am a woman under compulsion," Anne says. "I am locked in by the evidence to giving a verbal expression of what I know, what I've seen, what I've heard, what I've experienced by faith, what he [God] has said to me by his Word."[12]

Jill Briscoe says, "The Holy Spirit decides what gifts you have. You do not decide."[13] Our job as women of influence is discovery of those gifts. Ruth Tucker says the best evidence for using women in leadership roles is that we all, women as well as men, are required to live out in obedience the commands in the Bible like "Go and make disciples" (Mt 28:19) and "Preach the Word; be prepared in season and out of season;

correct, rebuke and encourage" (2 Tim 4:2).[14] God expects people of both genders to be obedient to his commands.

This question of a woman's role in leadership will probably never be settled to everyone's satisfaction. It would take this entire book just to open up the topic. We may never know all the answers, so it may be the best course of action to continue to ask questions even as we step out and influence. Gretchen Gaebelein Hull, in *Equal to Serve,* raises many thought-provoking questions that a woman of influence should seek to answer from the Bible so that she can be true to God and herself:

☐ What advice does the Bible have for us on our quest for approval?
☐ Is our tradition scriptural?
☐ Will you give up your rights to yourself and any entitlement to a certain position—and obey his call?
☐ Will you accept the authority of God?
☐ In the end, whose approval really matters most to you?

God's approval matters. That's why the woman of influence will not circumvent the Bible in order to lead. She will embrace God's Word in order to find her unique place of leadership.

Questions that have helped me find my unique place of leadership have included:

☐ What is the context of this question or this passage of Scripture? What was the culture then, and is this a specific command for a specific day and time or is this a command that crosses cultures and time periods?
☐ What is the whole counsel of God on this issue? The Bible is the best commentary on the Bible. I want to know from cover to cover what the Bible says, rather than looking for one verse just to prove my point.
☐ Can I gain more insight from a study of this issue by commentators and Bible scholars? historians? the original language?

Part of putting on the hat of leadership is being convinced of your theology of leadership.

Put On the Hat!

Feeling confident in Christ is an attitude you can put on. "Not that we are competent in ourselves to claim anything for ourselves, but our competence comes from God" (2 Cor 3:5). We are competent when we are in him. We may not *feel* qualified. We may not *feel* committed. We may not *feel* motivated—may not feel like wearing a hat of influence. But as you function according to the gifts and abilities God built into you, your feelings will catch up.

If you simply step out in obedience and see yourself as God sees you, God will see to it that you get all the training and resources you need! You'll have to find the right hat. He has a role created especially for you. Your individual influence counts. No matter how small it may seem to us, it's not small to God. A small thing from our side of eternity may be used by God in large ways.

This poem helps me see influence through God's eyes.

"Where shall I work today, dear Lord?"
And my love flowed warm and free.
He answered and said, "See that little place?
Tend that place for Me."
I answered and said, "Oh no, not there!
No one would ever see
No matter how well my work was done,
Not that little place for me!"
His voice, when He spoke, was soft and kind,
He answered me tenderly,
"Little one, search that heart of thine,
Are you working for them . . . or Me?
Nazareth was a little place . . . so was Galilee."[15]

Often big things grow out of obedience to small things. Fern Nichols was a mother and homemaker living in Poway, California, when her two older boys were entering a public school. She asked God for a concerned friend who would pray with her, and "Moms in Touch Ministry" was born. Ten years later, over 100,000 mothers in over forty-one countries gather to pray an hour a week for their children, the teachers and the educational system which their child attends. Fern humbly credits "just being available" as the reason God uses women like herself. "When we desire to abide in the vine daily, we never know what day He'll choose to change our life forever."[16]

Being open to the unique leadership role God has for you will change your life—and the lives of others as well. Your influence is unique, so . . . grab your hat.

Living It Out

Ask a more mature woman, who knows you fairly well, to take the Leadership Style Test for you. Have her insert your name (instead of "I prefer to work behind the scenes," it will be "Pam prefers to work behind the scenes"), and see if her results are the same as yours. Talk about the similarities and differences.

Chapter 3

A Woman
of Influence
Is Intimate
with God

O H, NO!" I SCREAMED AS I LOOKED AT THE GAS GAUGE IN DISBELIEF. IT
was one of those hectic, "terrible, horrible, no good, very bad
days." I had a "To Do" list the size of a phone book, and now
my car was sputtering to an abrupt halt on the freeway. It refused to
move despite my pleadings: "We're almost to the off ramp, you can at
least make it to there! Please move—just a little farther. Don't be out of
gas. Not here. Not now!" I was definitely out of gas.

Out of gas. That phrase rang in my head. *That's how I feel, Lord. I've
given and given so much lately. I'm running on empty.*

Walking down the freeway to the off ramp, I had plenty of time to
think about how hungry I had become for God. I tried rationalizing.
*God, you know I've been very busy—school, kids, work, ministry, the
house . . .* The words seemed so hollow.

In my mind, I recalled the words on a bookmark in my Bible: "My worth to God in public is what I am in private."

Oswald Chambers's comment repeated over and over in my head. I found myself walking to the cadence of his words. My worth to God . . . in public . . . is what I am . . . in private.

You're right, Lord. This past week, I have been feeding myself spiritually on about two minutes of devotional reading a day. I thought about how physically drained I would become if I ate only one Twinkie a day. No wonder my spiritual tank was on the red *E*, just like my car.

I really missed spending time with Jesus. Oh, I'd touch base with him throughout the day, but I longed for an extended time in his presence. I wanted to be quiet before him. I wanted a heart-to-heart time with my Savior and best friend. I wanted to sing and pray and listen.

Connecting with God

The word *intimacy* comes from the Latin *intimus,* which means innermost. God's desire is to let you and me in on his innermost thoughts. As we reflect on those, he becomes a mirror to our own soul.

Intimacy with God helps me know God better, but it also helps me know myself. You might feel you have to wait until heaven to truly know God, but John 17:3 says, "This is eternal life, that they may know you, the only true God." Eternal life begins the moment we are introduced to Jesus personally. God says, "Call to me and I will answer you and tell you great and unsearchable things you do not know"(Jer 33:3). The apostle Paul understood this concept. His heart cry is captured as he writes, "Whatever was to my profit I now consider loss for the sake of Christ. What is more, I consider everything a loss compared to the surpassing greatness of knowing Christ Jesus my Lord" (Phil 3:7-8). How can we women gain that same perspective?

Getting Reconnected

Some of us have fallen prey to lies about ourselves and our relationship to God. One lie I heard over and over as a university student was that because I am a woman, I am alienated from the God of the Bible. The argument told me and every other woman that because God chose to reveal himself using the personal pronoun *he,* all *shes* are alienated from God. Yes, God chose to reveal himself as *he,* but as you become connected to God you find that God transcends this gender debate.

Galatians 3:28 says that in Christ there is no male or female. In Genesis God says male and female are both made in his image. God understands me because I was made to reflect God. I am not an accident; my individual life has purpose. God longs to be connected with each human individual, both males and females. To be reconnected, all we have to do is ask. Just talk to God, as you would to a friend. Admit you are imperfect and you long to be accepted by him. Jesus came to earth to reconnect us to God; we need only receive the gift of his sacrifice on our behalf.

C. S. Lewis, a wonderful Oxford philosopher and writer, has one of his fictional characters explain that when people "are wholly His they will be more themselves than ever."[1] God unleashes us to be all we can be because he created us. I find freedom in being connected to my Creator.

God's creativity is available to you. Too often women feel there is a "right" way to learn about God. We can learn about him through many methods. God's Word, the Bible, is a love letter to you. Within its pages is everything you need to find a life of hope and meaning. Kay Arthur, author of the Precept Bible Studies, says, "Every child of God desperately needs a personal and intimate knowledge of the pure Word. . . . God gave us a lifetime and that's what it takes to mine the treasures of His Word."[2]

Each woman can build into her relationship with God by hearing, reading, studying and memorizing God's Word. Then she can plug back into God in prayer. I have found six simple methods that every woman can utilize to study the Bible for herself.

1. Be a news reporter. I loved my years as a journalist. In Journalism 101 we were taught a list of one-word questions to use in every interview: Who? What? Where? When? Why? How? You can open your Bible to any verse, ask these simple questions, write down the answers—and you will have learned the basics of that verse. The "how" is best used as an application: "How can I use what I've just learned?"

2. Be a psychologist. Make yourself an observer of a person in the Bible. Read and record the words he or she said and the actions he or she took. Then you can infer from that information what character traits he or she possesses. This is called a character study. The easiest way to accomplish a character study is to take a concordance, look up the person's name, then record every verse that has anything to do with this character. Read the stories in their context, then answer these five questions: What did _____ do? Who did _____ know? What did _____ say? What characteristic is described or implied? How can I become like _____?

3. Be a florist. I like to know the whole counsel of God on a topic. Just as a florist gathers beautiful flowers from around the world to create a stunning bouquet, you can gather verses on a theme from throughout the Bible. We always have questions that need answers. Searching out verses by topic is a way of gleaning as much information as possible on any subject.

You may have questions like "Why is there pain and suffering?" "How can I deal with my fears?" "What does God say about divorce?" When those questions come to mind, it is time for a theme study. Again consult your handy concordance, now available on computer disk! Look up every word or phrase that could possibly be related to your question.

For example, for the question about pain, I would look up *pain, suffering, persecution*—and also some possible solutions like *endure, long-suffering, steadfast* and so on. I would record the key thought of each passage. Then I'd look for patterns, repeated words or ideas, commands and promises. I would then draw conclusions about my own life based on that new knowledge.

4. Be a linguist. Words can be fascinating. The Bible was first written in three languages: Hebrew, Greek and a little Aramaic. As a result, words can lose a little of their pizzazz when translated to English. Hebrew is a language of pictures. Studying the word development of a Hebrew word will give us a visual aid opening up its meaning. Greek, on the other hand, is very exact. To find word meanings, I use *Strong's Exhaustive Concordance, The Theological Wordbook of the Old Testament* and *The Expository Dictionary of New Testament Words,* which have detailed instructions in their preface. I check the outcome of my study with good commentaries, because the highlights of key word meanings are usually covered in a commentary.

5. Be an English student. No doubt some of you reading this book were a whiz at outlining in elementary school. By taking a selected passage and breaking it down in outline form, you can glean key principles for daily living. The first step is to write out the verse(s) so that the most important points are to the left and the lesser details fall to the right. Key words or phrases can be highlighted or boldfaced. For example, Colossians 1:10-12 could be written:

And we PRAY
   this in order that
      YOU MAY LIVE A LIFE WORTHY OF THE LORD
         and
      MAY PLEASE HIM
     in every way:
      bearing fruit
      in every good work,
      growing
         in the knowledge of God,
       being strengthened with all power
         according to HIS glorious might
    so that you may have

great endurance
and
patience,
and
joyfully giving thanks
to the Father,
who has qualified you to share
in the inheritance
of the saints
in the kingdom of light.

From writing the verse in outline form, I can clearly see several key issues to commit to prayer. I might want to study the key points first so I can be more specific in my application. My study outline might look like this:

MY PRAYER FOR A WORTHY WALK

I. What Pleases God
  A. Bearing fruit
  B. Growing in knowledge of God
  C. Being strengthened with all power
    1. According to HIS glorious might
II. Results of Pleasing God
  A. Great endurance
  B. Patience
  C. Joyfully giving thanks
    1. Why I can be thankful
      a. God is my Father
      b. God qualified me to share in inheritance

This could be my quiet time outline for an entire week. I could do theme and word studies to try to figure out just what Paul was praying for the believers in Colossae. I could then apply these to prayers for myself and the ones I seek to influence.

    6. *Be an artist.* In the play *The Quilters*, one character says as she

stitches, "Each block is different. Each pattern has a thread of some-body's life running through it. You'll see my thread in there from time to time with all the others . . . my memories, my hopes, my dreams, my prayers."[3]

One artistic friend of mine struggled with her daily quiet time. She felt pressured to make her journal perfect. She lamented that she didn't get the "right" answers when using more intellectual study methods. She found herself dreading her time with God rather than looking forward to meeting him. "I want to grow in my knowledge of God. And I really want to know God's Word. But all the methods I've tried make me feel distant from him."

"Treat your quiet time journal like a sketch pad," I suggested. "Write down a special verse each day or just a word or two that is meaningful. Marking up your Bible creatively might help you visually understand a passage better. You could mark promises with rainbows. Special verses are marked in my Bible with hearts and asterisks. You can use a variety of symbols to decorate a passage and get a grasp of main topics or key ideas. In your journal, write down how it touched you or applies to you. Then depict it in an artistic way. God made you an artist, so he'll speak to your artistic heart."

Donna, a woman who designs beautiful hand-stitched quilts, studied Genesis for a year in a small-group Bible study. Inspired by God's creative work, she stitched a quilt depicting the seven days of creation. The Word of God had gone in through her head, down through her heart and out through her hand. Art is an overflow of a strong connection to God.

A Personal Connection

I am connected to God by his personalness. In Matthew 23:37 Jesus weeps and longs to gather Jerusalem as a mother hen gathers her chicks. God tells me in Jeremiah 29:11, "I know the plans I have for you . . . plans to prosper you and not to harm you, plans to give you hope and a future." God reveals himself as a personal being—not a force, not a philosophy, not even a religion. God is personal and knowable. God's arms are always open, wanting to embrace me—the choice is mine.

On January 31, 1993, Nancy and Dave Mankin were reclining in their hammocks and enjoying an evening of quiet conversation on their missionary base in Panama. Suddenly three men rushed in and pointed automatic rifles at them. They screamed demands at Dave, but Dave couldn't understand them.

Nancy prayed. Instantly, she remembered the hostage training she had taken four years prior at a New Tribes conference. She remembered that the most important thing is to remain calm. The first thirty to sixty seconds are the most important, because that is when most people are killed.

Her heart quieted. Nancy calmly asked the men to repeat the instructions. She explained that her husband would try to cooperate but that he didn't understand. The men calmly repeated their requests. This time Dave could comprehend.

Nancy also remembered her instructions to maintain eye contact with her would-be captors. The phrase "Make yourself human to them" rang in her head. As much as possible, Nancy tried to treat the guerrillas as humans, praying they would treat her the same.

Suddenly another man entered their home. This man was much more wild-looking and agitated. He yelled for phone numbers and money. He pushed Nancy up the stairway. One of the first men accompanied her also. Fearing rape, she climbed only a few steps and reached for her purse on the landing. The wild man yelled at her to go upstairs.

Nancy calmly turned to the first man, whom she had come to trust somewhat, handed him the purse and said, "No, I am not going up the stairs." Amazingly, the men parted and allowed her to come back down.

Nancy continued to gather the supplies the men asked for and packed a suitcase for Dave. One of the men told her to say her goodbys. She leaned toward Dave and said, "I'm going to kiss you goodby."

Dave answered, "Do you think they'll let you?"

Nancy calmly replied, "They said, 'Say your goodbys.' " Then the two kissed and Dave was marched out into the night.

Quick decisions were necessary to ensure the safety of all of the missionaries and children left on the compound. Supernatural peace again entered Nancy's heart. Just two weeks prior, she had asked Dave to explain to her what to do if guerrillas came, took the men and left the women. Dave thought the question odd because, in his opinion, probably all would be taken or no one would be left alive. But Nancy persisted and Dave explained a plan of escape downriver. It was that plan that carried the women and children to safety.

Nancy credits God with her ability to maintain a cool head in such horrific circumstances. She also credits God with the supernatural peace that comes through a personal connection with God. In a very private and individual way, God has enabled her to keep going on, day after day, as she and the other family members await news of their men. As of the writing of this chapter, the men have still not been released.

Nancy clings to a quote from Hannah Whitall Smith's *Safe Within Your Love:*

> I feel just like a little chick who has run out of a storm and under his mother's wings and is safe there. I hear the raging of the storm and I am utterly unable to comprehend it or measure the damage it is doing. But I am safe under His wings. He can manage the dark storm but I cannot. Why then should I worry or be anxious? . . . When I feel hopeless or fear, I know I need to get back under His Wings.[4]

An Emotional Connection

When I was pregnant with my third son, one of my best friends, Tamera, was also pregnant. After church one Sunday, Tamera sensed I needed a break. We packed up both of our families and headed to a park for a picnic. Our conversation turned to how we handle adversity.

"You always just go on," Tamera said with a smile. She didn't need to say any more. She had already shared with me the major and minor trials that had accompanied the births of each of her three sons. Tamera was now expecting a baby girl.

A few weeks later, late at night, I got a call from her husband, Tony. Their baby girl had been born, but the doctors had told them that she had a terminal condition that was not compatible with life. Her sweet baby girl was going to die.

The next few days I walked through this valley with my friend. Sooner than I was ready for it, I got the call: "She's home with Jesus. I rocked my baby into Jesus' arms."

Tamera wept. I wept. Jesus wept.

Often, we forget that Jesus too felt deeply—feels deeply. When his dear friend Lazarus died, he knew the pain of Mary and Martha, Lazarus's sisters. Each said to him, "Lord, if you had been here, my brother wouldn't have died." The Bible says that as Jesus stood by the tomb of his friends "he was deeply moved in spirit and troubled" (Jn 11:33). He knew he was going to raise Lazarus from the dead. He knew he would turn bad into good, yet he was still moved. God incarnate was emotionally connected to the pain.

I was by Tamera's side through the days of funeral preparation and the memorial service. I witnessed how God emotionally connected with her in a way I could not. Nothing could have prepared me for the note I saw on her door as I carried in food after the funeral.

"Shall we accept good from God, and not trouble?" (Job 2:10).

That verse captured the strength I saw in Tamera from the moment her world crashed in around her. She didn't mouth the words. She walked the road by faith. Tamera was choosing to believe in God's character even when her life seemed pitch black. Through the expected days of torrential grief ahead, she kept choosing to thank God for being God.

Some days, her grief would overwhelm her. "I want to believe this will be turned into good, Pam."

"I do too. I'll loan you my faith to believe," I offered.

"I'll take it! I want to hang on . . . to life . . . to God . . . to hope." She didn't know why this had happened or how she was ever going to go on with life, but she kept tenaciously holding on to God. She kept the connection open. Just about one year from the day of her precious daughter's death, new life again came into her arms. Tamera delivered a healthy baby girl!

An Attentive Connection

God hears. His ear is attentive to our hearts when we seek to commune with him. When we pray, we realize just how attentive God is to us. Sometimes when you are praying, your mind may wander. Instead of heaping guilt on yourself for a lack of self-will, simply pray through the area that's on your mind. These are areas of your life that God wants to address now! Satan may be trying to tempt you, and God is getting your attention. Or this may be an area of selfishness that God wants to free you from. The best recourse is to pray through them, then go back to your original concerns.

My prayer life is more meaningful if I look for opportunities to praise and adore God, not for his sake, but for my own. He wants to hear my list of cares, not because he needs to hear them but because I need to tell him. The movie *Shadowlands* is the love story of C. S. Lewis. Lewis married late in life, and soon after, his new wife, Joy, was diagnosed with cancer. Lewis prayed and prayed as her health deteriorated. A theological colleague commented that surely all of Lewis's prayers had changed the plan of God. Lewis replied, "I pray because the need flows out of me all the time . . . it [prayer] doesn't change God, it changes me."[5]

One change that a connection with God will bring is wisdom. Before every big decision in my life, I have taken an extended time away to spend with God. Before Bill and I married, before sending Bill back to school, before we decided on seminary, before we had each of our three boys, before we left the youth ministry, before we accepted a pastorate, before we built a house, before I returned to school, before every book we set aside a day to pray.

Bill and I set aside special days to pray before major transitions in our boys' lives such as starting school or entering puberty. And each August, before the boys begin school, we set aside one day as our "Learner and Leader" day. We do something fun as a family; then, over a meal, we negotiate privileges and responsibilities for the next year. Bill and I also choose a special gift for each son that will encourage the leadership trait he will be working on for the next year. We give each son his gift, along with a verbal blessing, and then we pray for him.

One of my role models in mothering calls her family together to fast and pray if one of her children is experiencing extra stress or having to make a big decision. Every one of her four children has a strong relationship with Jesus. All of them spent a portion of their adult lives in full-time ministry and are now using their careers to further God's agenda in the world.

A Unique Connection

I also use regular mornings or afternoons away to keep my relationship with Christ fresh. On my "dates with Jesus," I always take the same things: a Bible, my prayer notebook, my journal and a concordance. I may also take a book on a particular subject, an informative or inspiring article, my daily planner and a devotional book. I usually spend time closing my heart to distractions by writing them out in a journal and finding verses to salve the cries of my heart. I usually have a topic that I want to research or a decision I need to spend time in the Word about. I also take this opportunity to have my own personal worship service, including singing and extended prayer. Each time is different, but each time I am renewed. Sometimes I get away to a mountain cabin, a park or beach. Other times I am most comforted by my own familiar surroundings. More than anything, I am comforted by God's Word.

In our hectic world, God's presence is a haven for sanity. I look for quiet moments throughout my day to refocus my heart on God: right before I rise and before I doze off at night, in the shower and as I blow-dry my hair—they can all be times for a "holy huddle" with God. I love to lap swim and take walks because I can shut away the outside world and focus on God. I use these times to think through my life from his perspective.

My prayer connection is enhanced with memorization. After twenty-four hours, you may accurately remember 5 percent of what your hear, 15 percent of what you read, 35 percent of what you study, 57 percent of what you see and hear, but 100 percent of what you memorize.[6] If I study and memorize, I can then "marinate" in the Word. When I marinate chicken for the grill, the chicken still maintains its personality. It's 100 percent chicken, but it no longer smells or tastes the same. As we submerge ourselves in the Word, we are still ourselves—but with the savory flavor of one who has been in God's presence. A woman of influence is wise to protect these quiet connections.

While all these principles will enhance our relationship with God, they are not a magic checklist. Each woman of influence needs to find her own intimacy rhythm. Because the goal is intimacy, not legalistic ritual, every woman is free to develop her relationship with God uniquely. The blend of ingredients may change with time or circumstance.

One friend of mine with small children shared that she felt guilty because she didn't get up an hour before her family and spend time with God. She was functioning on less than five hours of sleep as it was, and she found it impossible to carve the time out during the day.

"Why does the time have to be in a single one-hour block?" I asked.

"That's just how I was taught it was supposed to be."

I explained to her that often I prefer to spread out my intimate moments with the Lord. "First thing in the morning, I read a small section of Scripture. I claim a phrase or a verse as mine for the day. On my mirror are verses I am working on memorizing. I repeat them as I blow-dry my hair and put on my makeup. Over lunch, I like to do my Bible study. In the car, I listen to praise music and I pray. In the evening, after the kids are in bed, I journal my thoughts and note any specific requests or answers to prayer in my prayer notebook. At the end of the day my heart is drawn to Christ in worship, because I feel I have been in his presence all day."

Everyone should include all the basic principles, but the amount and blend are different with each of us. I ask God what rhythm he wants me to have to maintain a strong connection with him. My plan has been a nice rhythm for me for several years. I am open to changing the pattern, because I am open to Jesus changing me. *Communing with Jesus is not something you do—it is a place where you dwell. Intimacy is being with Jesus.*

A Nurturing Connection

God wants to nurture our relationship with him. As God nurtures us, we can often encourage others in their relationship with God. As we open up our hearts and share, we strengthen one another's connections to God. Teresa Muller is a dear friend of mine. She is also a songwriter and recording artist. A song she wrote ministered to me long before God brought her into my life.

Teresa was coming home from a hospital visit to her mother. She was concerned about her mom; her heart was heavy and she was talking to God about her feelings. As she prayed, a melody came clearly into her mind. She then began weaving her feelings and the melody together into a song.

You are the Rock of my salvation,
You are the strength of my life,
You are my hope and my inspiration,
Lord, unto you do I cry.

I believe in you, believe in you,
for your faithful love to me.
You have been my help in time of need.
Lord, unto you do I cleave.[7]

Teresa felt drawn to God. Her heart seemed lighter and more hopeful
in God's ability to see her through the current situation and her future.

"You Are the Rock of My Salvation" was a song I sang through a
depression after a move. It was a song I sang as I prayed all night for
my friend Tamera in her crisis. "You Are the Rock of My Salvation" has
encouraged me before speaking engagements, during exams and
throughout personal trials. I can't read music, but my heart can sing
because a women of influence like Teresa opened up her relationship
with Jesus and let me in. Teresa, too, had discovered that her worth to
God in public was what she was in private.

Just a Touch

One woman was desperate for a connection to God. She was very ill
with a menstrual disorder. She continually hemorrhaged. She was weak
from the blood loss and even weaker from the doctors' mistreatment.
She also felt desperately lonely. Her condition caused her to be an
outcast in her society. The people who had once been her friends now
turned away when they saw her coming. They saw her condition as
being her fault, so she was not allowed to eat with, converse with or
even walk within a few feet of anyone. Everyone thought she had
somehow brought her problems on herself.

But one day, her desperation pushed her over the line of social and
religious customs. She pushed her way through the crowd. Her eyes
were fixed on one face. She was going to get help for her problem,
and she was going to do whatever it took. She'd heard about a man
who had solutions to every kind of problem. And that man was only
a few feet away from her. She thought, *If I can only touch the hem of*

his garment, I will be well. Her frail hand reached through the throng gathered around him and—just a touch—her finger reached the edge of his cloak. At that moment, the bleeding stopped.

The swarming crowd carried the man out of her grasp. But Jesus turned and asked, "Who touched me?"

His disciples were outraged at the question. How were they supposed to know? After all, this was a crowd pressing in from every side.

Timidly the woman fell at Jesus' feet and said, "It was I." Jesus answered, "Daughter, your faith has healed you" (Mk 5:34). His power had healed her infirmity, but his personal words to her healed her heart. For in that instant, all the crowd knew she was now clean and invited back into the society that had formerly alienated her. Just a touch will keep you connected; a touch will give you the power to live above life's circumstances; a touch—a connection with God—will influence your heart and then in turn influence others.

How's your connection? Reach out today. Catch a fresh hold on Christ's garment of love for you.

Living It Out
Choose one new idea from the following list to try out each day this week.

30 Intimacy Ideas: Growing in Your Unique Relationship with God

1. Make your prayer more concrete by writing it out as a letter to Jesus.

2. Go on a prayer walk, talking to the Lord as you walk along.

3. Pray through Scripture. Write out verses and personalize them with your name. For example, Psalm 84:11 (NASB): "No good thing does he withhold from Pam who walks uprightly."

4. Make a poster with one of your favorite verses on it. You may

choose to take a photo and have it developed into a poster, then write the verse on the poster.

5. Read the Bible through, mark it up and give it as a gift to a child. As you read, try to picture God through his or her eyes. Mark verses that you think will help the child in the transitions to come.

6. Make "devotion baskets" and place them in several areas of your home. Decorate each basket and place in it a pen, a Bible, a devotional or inspirational book and paper.

7. Sing for your entire time with God. You may want to try your hand at songwriting too.

8. Dance before the Lord like David. Maybe you enjoy Jewish dancing or ballet. Dedicate your talent to Christ.

9. Begin a miracle scrapbook. Keep photos and mementos that remind you of God's grace to you.

10. Write down every sin that continues to haunt you. Then write 1 John 1:9 over the list. This is a visual of God's blotting out your sin. Destroy the list—God has.

11. Write out a Philippians 4:8 list. What is lovely to you, worthy of praise, excellent and so on?

12. Pray in a way you are not accustomed to. Try on your knees, or prone, or stand with your face to the heavens and your hands raised up in worship.

13. Prepare a way to speak out for Jesus. Write a letter to a friend or create a greeting card. Write to a newspaper or create an ad campaign.

14. Give a gift to God. Donate anonymously to someone in need.

15. Go to a Christian bookstore and try out a new Bible-study tool.

16. Praise Jesus from A to Z. "Jesus, you are amazing, beautiful . . ."

17. Try repeating every verse you have memorized, in order, from Genesis to Revelation. Stop at the first book you don't have a verse from, and learn one.

18. Make a list notebook. List areas of hurt or need in your life. As

you come to a verse that shows how God can meet the need, write it down. You're creating your own book of promises.

19. Read your favorite hymn. Find the verse it was based on and try to find out the story behind it.

20. Reread your sermon notes from last Sunday, or read ahead on the passage to be covered this Sunday.

21. Think back and picture your life before you were a Christian. What has Jesus "saved" you from?

22. Write your own subtitles over each chapter number in your Bible. Use a different version of the Bible from time to time.

23. Fast from food, TV or a hobby in order to spend a longer time with God.

24. Write about your relationship with God from a different point of view. For example, my teen son might say, "Mom, she has a radical walk with Jesus. She gets so stoked (excited). Awesome, dude."

25. Memorize one of the prayers in the Bible. Mary's prayer in Luke 1:46-55 is a good start.

26. Write and thank those people in your life who helped you grow in your walk this year, or write to mentors from the past.

27. Write out a list of theological questions you'd like answered. Choose one and start researching it.

28. Go early to church. Walk the rows, sit in different places and pray for others who will sit there later.

29. Exercise to Christian music.

30. Tell one person who doesn't know Christ that you do know and love him.

Chapter 4

A Woman
of Influence
Is Idealistic

A WOMAN IN A BIG HAT STOOD BEFORE THE CROWD. SHE WAS SINGLE, and she was single-minded. "It is the individual who counts. One man, Luther, started the Reformation in Germany. One man, Moses, led the children of Israel out of Egypt. One man, Paul, carried the gospel to the Roman empire. God always works through the individual."[1] This woman's idealism has affected the church as much as anyone of her time.

Henrietta Mears was a schoolteacher from the Midwest who landed at Hollywood Presbyterian Church in 1928. She ran the Sunday-school department and turned it into a huge success. She also saw a need for high-quality, grade-appropriate material, so she and a friend wrote what was needed. This curriculum became the core of Gospel Light Publishing House. She saw a need to train young people, so her college department swelled and hundreds of lives were changed. She also believed that camping provided a wonderful atmosphere for students to do some serious reflecting, so she founded Forest Home Conference Center, one the United States' most respected camping facilities.

She challenged individuals to influence. One night after a college-age group's sharing time, Henrietta stood to her feet and said:

This is the most ridiculous testimony time I think I have ever heard! All we have been talking about is silly little things that don't amount to a hill of beans. Have we lost sight of why we are here?

There hasn't been one word about winning the nations for Christ. How about these great campuses in this area? Hasn't anything been done out at UCLA this week? Hasn't anyone witnessed to a student at USC?

God weeps over these lost students, and we come here to talk about trifles. St. Paul dreamed about kingdoms brought to Christ. Knox cried, "Give me Scotland or I die." Luther wept over Germany.[2]

After World War II, Henrietta gathered former students, now leaders, for a recommissioning and vision-setting gathering. The group represented over fifty Christian organizations. Some of those attending were Richard Halverson, who went on to be chaplain of the U.S. Senate; Louis Evans Jr., who went on to pastor several growing churches, including one in Washington, D.C.; and Bill Bright, who just a few years later started Campus Crusade for Christ, which is now an international organization.

Henrietta was just one woman, but she had a big dream. Once she said, "There is no magic in small plans. When I consider my ministry, I think of the world. Anything less than that would not be worthy of Christ nor of his will for my life."[3] How could one single, unpretentious woman be so fearless in her ability to believe God for great things? Seems impossible!

Some days I wonder if I have a great plan—or *any* plan. If you can't figure out where unmatched socks disappear when washed—or where you put your car keys—is it possible to be part of God's great plan for using your life to change the *world?* Have no fear—it is possible.

No Fear

In San Diego, a sports lifestyle brand started marketing thought-provoking sayings. Overnight the company sprang to international success. It was because the company caught what we all want: "No Fear!"—the ability to be courageous in the face of life's circumstances. One of their T-shirts says, "You miss 100% of the shots you don't take." Another says, "If you're not living on the edge then you are taking up too much space." Their catalog captures the dilemma of an idealist: "Think of yourself as invincible. Believe everything is yours for a price. Some will call it foolish and blame it on the innocence of youth . . . others will just call it courage."

Idealism is the ability to envision a dream and imagine the steps needed to achieve it. Idealists are optimistic. They envision life as it can be rather than as it is. They want more than the status quo. Idealists have hope rooted in the person of God. The clearer your vision of God, the clearer your vision will be of yourself and life.

Idealists are sometimes thought of as "so heavenly minded that they are no earthly good." Idealists see life as an adventure. In *Man of La Mancha,* Don Quixote is treated as a fool and madman because he dares to dream the impossible dream. But without those who dream the impossible, we'd all live in a much darker world. Without idealists, many of us would still be riding in the back of the bus, many would have no voice at the polls, many would still be in chains and rags and treated as less than human. Without idealists, no woman would have been educated, been allowed to vote, owned a business or property, held a political office. Idealists make the world a better place, not because all of the dreams are fulfilled but because with each dream one step of progress is made, one more need is fulfilled, one more glimpse of hope is given.

Hope is the key ingredient of sanity in an insane world. I find hope in God's Word. Years ago, each time I would hit a tough circumstance or feel depressed, I'd search for a verse that would encourage me. Soon, several pages in my Bible became dog-eared. Then I hit a very lonely time after a move to a new city. I called a friend, Mary, and in the course of our conversation she shared a principle she'd just heard at a leadership conference.

Mary asked me what attribute of God I was not believing. Her words challenged me. I knew that I needed to get a fresh view of the God whom I said I loved and who I thought loved me. I strung together the verses off the dog-eared pages and personalized God's Word to my heart. It is really a message from God's heart to my own. Since that time, these verses have encouraged me to step out, try the improbable and believe God for the impossible. No matter how dismal or overwhelming the circumstance, reading verses like these puts life in proper perspective. God's very character can elevate you out of the pit. This letter now hangs in my home to remind me daily of who God is and of his personal love to me. Below is my letter, from God's perspective—his words personalized for me and shared with you:

Dear Pam,

Nothing is impossible for Me. I am able to do immeasurably more than all you can ask or think. In Me all things were created, in heaven and on earth, visible and invisible . . . thrones . . . powers . . . rulers . . . authorities. All things were created by Me and I am before all things and in Me all things hold together.

Mine is the greatness and the power and the glory and the majesty and the splendor . . . I am exalted as head over all. Wealth and honor come from Me. In my hands are strength and power to exalt . . . Nothing on earth is my equal!

It is not by [your] might nor by [your] power but by my spirit . . . I know when you sit down and when you rise; I perceive your thoughts from afar . . . I am familiar with all your ways. Before a word is on

*your tongue I know it completely . . . You cannot flee from my
presence. If you go up to the heavens, I am there; if you make your bed
in the depths, I am there. If you rise on the wings of the dawn, if you
settle on the far side of the sea, even there my hand will guide you, my
right hand will hold you fast . . . even the darkness is as light to Me . . .*

*I stretch out the heavens like a canopy and spread them out like a
tent to dwell in . . . I measure the waters of the earth in the hollow of
my hand, and with the breadth of my hand I mark off the heavens.*

*I am the Creator. I am the Wonderful Counselor, the Mighty God,
the Everlasting Father, the Prince of Peace. I am the Alpha and Omega,
. . . the Beginning and the End.*

*I am immortal and dwell in unapproachable light . . . [yet I tell
you:] Approach my throne of grace with confidence, so that you may
receive mercy and find grace to help in time of need.*

*I do not grow tired or weary; I have understanding no one can
fathom . . . My judgments are unsearchable, my paths . . . beyond
tracing out! My thoughts are precious and vast are the sum of them!
No one fully understands my mind . . . No one instructed Me. No one
taught Me the right way . . . No one can compare . . .*

*I hem you in before and behind . . . be convinced that neither
death nor life, neither angels nor demons, neither present nor the
future nor any powers, neither height not depth nor anything else in
all creation can separate you from my love.*[4]

Focusing In on God

Just as a camera can record a scenic view, so the Bible records snapshots
of who God is. Our minds are finite and God is infinite; yet he chose
to reveal himself in snapshots so that we could know him more
personally. God reveals a lot about himself through the names he calls
himself. If we can carry these pictures around with us, we can
accomplish much more of what we dream.

One of my favorite names of God is *Jehovah-raah,* "The Lord is my shepherd." I grew up on a Suffolk sheep farm in eastern Idaho. Year after year, we would watch the tiny lambs being born, and my brother, my sister and I would each get to choose a 4-H lamb from the "bummer" lambs. These lambs were either rejected or orphaned and needed tender loving care from us to survive. I loved watching my grandfather tramp through the snow to lovingly wrap the tiny lambs in a blanket and place them in the warm lambing shed. My mother and grandmother would prepare baby bottles, and then each of us children would get to hold the tiny lambs and feed them like a baby. That was the tender part of shepherding.

Those days were short. Long were the days of worming, shearing and herding the flock. Even longer were the scorching-hot days when we three kids would clean out the shed and the stockyard and work the hay and grain harvest. But the nights were even longer. Many nights my father, grandfather and brother would sit in a freezing pickup truck in snowsuits, armed with guns to scare off the wild dogs, coyotes and wolves.

When God says he is my shepherd, I know that there will be times when he tenderly holds and nourishes me. But there will be many more times that he dresses my wounds, herds me in the right direction and shears off the sin that so easily entangles me. He'll even clean up after I make a mess of my life, and he is ever standing guard over me.

At ten, my first year in 4-H, I had a little lamb that I named Bunny because in the early spring he loved to hop from rock to rock like a rabbit. Bunny and I went everywhere together for eight months. I'd hold Bunny. I'd card his soft, lanolin-coated wool. I'd feed and water him. I'd practice showing him. Bunny and I went on long walks together.

Bunny was my friend. He did well in the county fair. But then came auction day. As I knelt in the noisy ring, I couldn't fully comprehend what was taking place. Then I heard the gavel slam down and the auctioneer announce, "Sold!" A man motioned for Bunny and me to go down a chute, and someone yelled, "Let him go!"

I started to cry. "No, I can't." So they came and took Bunny out of my hands. Bunny was frightened. He didn't recognize the strange voices or the rough treatment. I turned and buried my tearful face in my dad's jacket. My mom's arm went around me. I knew I couldn't get Bunny back—not ever.

About eight years later, I sat in a quiet dorm room and read the words from John 10 about Jesus being the good shepherd. Verses 27 and 28 seemed to be in bold print: "My sheep listen to my voice; I know them, and they follow me. I give them eternal life, and they shall never perish; no one can snatch them out of my hand."

My eyes welled up. I would never have the fate of my lamb, Bunny. I was God's lamb, and no one could snatch me out of his hand. I would never be separated from his care—not ever. Knowing I'm secure in the Good Shepherd's care gives me more courage, even when things get rough and I can't see the purpose.

His Name Is Wonderful

Throughout the book of John, Jesus keeps saying, "I am." "I am the bread of life," "I am the light of the world," "I am the good shepherd," "I am the living water," "I am the door," "I am the way, the truth and the life," "I am the vine." Whatever your needs are today, Jesus says he himself is the answer to those needs.

Whenever I am feeling vulnerable and weak, I go to the Psalms. There the poet's pen quenches my fears with beautiful word-pictures of the person of God. My idealism returns as I read how God surrounds me like a shield, that he is my rock, my fortress, my stronghold, my bulwark. Being the mother of three boys, I have firsthand experience with these portraits of war.

A few summers ago, the boys and I studied swords, shields and other defenses against enemy attacks. We wanted to re-create some of these instruments of defense to play away a long, hot afternoon. But as we studied, I realized my impressions of these things were based more on cartoons than on the Bible!

When God says he is our *shield,* he doesn't mean some tiny tin plate with a fancy crest. A shield in David's time was heavy; it wrapped around three sides of a person and was big enough for a large warrior to hide behind. The only ways to get hurt in battle were to be out from behind the shield or to be running in retreat and get hit from behind! Everything that this fallen world may send my way has to go through the character of God and his loving plan for me first. That's my kind of shield!

The *rock* means a solid place, high enough to give perspective. It was usually there that the stronghold or fortress was built. Cities in the Old Testament were self-sufficient, so that when attack came, the walls would enclose the inhabitants in safety and they would have all the necessities of life, like food and water. When I am resting in God and his character to fight my battles, I have everything I need to survive.

Finally, when the enemy of my life hails against me, I need to run into my *bulwark.* A fortress often had tall, usually circular towers at its corners. In the towers were small slits, each just large enough for the shaft of a well-aimed arrow to be shot out through it. From this vantage point, archers could clearly see the enemy approaching, yet be protected from harm while preparing their response to the attack. God is the only safe place I can run to, in order to gain the wisdom and insight to form a battle plan for my life.

Not only are we outwardly protected by God; we are protected by his indwelling Holy Spirit. The Spirit is our "pledge" from God (2 Cor 1:22 NASB). The word *pledge* is the same word used for a deposit or down payment. It was also used to describe an engagement ring.[5] God made a down payment of love by giving us the indwelling Holy Spirit. The indwelling of the Spirit changes us from the inside out.

God by his very character is able to be all we need. Mary Slessor knew God that way. As a young woman, she paddled her canoe into the jungles of Calabar (now Nigeria). She was headed further inland to a tribe of cannibals. She had already spent years working against the evils of tribal superstition as well as exploitation brought by white traders. The traders had brought rum and guns to the people but had brought them no light, no hope, no help. As she paddled she thought, "Who am I, a weak woman, to face wild savages alone?"

But she knew God. In *Our Faithful God: Answers to Prayer* she writes: My life is one long daily, hourly, record of answered prayer. For physical health, for . . . guidance given marvelously, for errors and dangers averted, for enmity to the gospel subdued, for food provided at the exact hour needed, for everything that goes to make up life and my poor service, I can testify with full and often wonder-stricken awe that I believe God answers prayer.[6]

Her relationship with God helped her battle the superstitions of the day. The most brutal was the custom of throwing newborn twins to the wild animals because it was thought that twins were a curse. She took these children into her own home and raised them as her own, and through the years she took in many more children besides.

She begged God for wisdom on how to combat the ongoing bloodshed between tribes. One day, a shriek rang out in the village. A tree had fallen on the chief's son and killed him. Because death was always connected to some curse, a neighboring tribe was blamed. Prisoners were rounded up for execution. Mary held an elaborate funeral for the chief's son, then sat vigil with the prisoners waiting on death row. After two weeks, the chief let the prisoners go. It was the first time in the history of the tribe that bloodshed had been averted.

At age sixty-seven, she finally succumbed to the malaria that had plagued her on and off throughout her thirty-eight years in Calabar. She was surrounded by a large crowd of Christian men and women, her now grown adopted children with children of their own. Tribespeople in Calabar mourned the loss of the woman who wrote in the margin of her Bible: "God and one are always a majority."[7]

Who Are You, Dad?

Nothing in your self-concept or your past is too big to keep you from reaching the goals God has for you. As we see God as he is, we will be able to see ourselves as he sees us, as women of influence. We are chosen, gifted, accepted by our Abba-Father. I believe there is a leader inside every woman, screaming to get out and change her world. God can free you!

For most of my father's life he has struggled with alcoholism. He is a goodhearted man who has been wounded and carries a lot of emotional baggage. He sought to drown the pain with a bottle. However, alcohol not only drowns the pain—it drowns the person. His good heart and gentle nature became bitter and calloused. The man who desired to always be there for his kids, and who often greatly sacrificed to do so, soon found himself emotionally absent from their lives.

His love for me was marred by his behavior. On my thirteenth birthday, I waited for him to stop drinking and start celebrating, but he passed out instead. As a teen, I tried denying that my dad had a problem. But it's not normal to fear that your dad will stagger down the hall to meet your date. It's not normal to rescue your mom from threats of violence. It's not normal to sit on your dad's chest all night, singing to him, to keep him from hanging himself in the garage. I finally resorted to avoidance, thinking that if I didn't see the problem it wouldn't be so bad—but it was. I couldn't move away and forget that I had a dad. My heart was attached to him. I loved him; he was my dad!

My feelings for my father were so mixed. At times he was a wonderful father. He provided well for our family. He would drive long distances to take me to dance recitals and gymnastics meets. He bragged about my accomplishments and told me he loved me. But sometimes he wounded me deeply. He didn't want to, but alcohol stole his ability to express love and be dependable.

In junior college I recommitted my life to Jesus. God, in his love, started to teach me about himself. I learned that I was a daughter of the King and that God wanted me to cry out to him, "*Abba,* Father" (Gal 4:6). *Abba* is an intimate word meaning Daddy. God wants us to call him Daddy!

By an act of my will, day after day, I have chosen to believe God's description of himself. And in believing that I am secure in my Abba-Father's love, I have found the power to forgive, love and extend unconditional grace to my earthly father. Because my Father in heaven has drawn me closer to himself, I have drawn closer to my own dad. It is my Father in heaven who gave me the ability to see and respond to the best in my dad who raised me.

You too may have some wound in your past that has colored your view of God or your view of yourself. You can be free as you allow God to be *Abba* to you.

God Is Reliable

We can all step out and believe God. One of my favorite chapters in the Bible is Genesis 15, where God makes a covenant with Abram.

God asked Abram to bring a heifer, a goat, a ram, a dove and a pigeon. Abram cut them in two and placed them end to end. In biblical times, when a covenant was made it was a very solemn commitment. There were no loopholes in the agreement. If you made a covenant, you would lock arms with the other person and walk down through the sliced-open animals. The blood of the animals would splash up and stain your skin and clothes. By doing this, you were saying, "If I fail to keep this covenant with you, you may do to me what has been done to these animals." It was a life-and-death decision.

God knew Abram was human and would err, so he put Abram to sleep and walked through the animals himself, in the form of a smoking firepot and a blazing torch. He made a covenant with himself. If he fails to keep his promises, he will cease to exist. We know by his very character that he is eternal and immortal and cannot cease to exist;

therefore, we can conclude that it is impossible for him to break a promise. We can put feet to our faith—*God is reliable!*

Stepping Out on a Promise

One woman, compelled by her heart, believed that the world could be a better place and that God wanted her to step out and do something to reach that ideal. She regularly took the risk of leading slaves through the Underground Railroad to find freedom in the North.

On one trip, she stopped at a sympathizer's home to feed and house her weary band. When she knocked, a stranger answered and said her friend was no longer around. Fearing capture, she prayed to God for a place to safely shelter her refugees. Dawn was breaking, so time was of the essence. She remembered a swamp nearby, and, carrying twin babies in a basket, she led the tired crew to the rushes and told them to lie down in the wet, cold marsh. Then she prayed for God's deliverance.

She feared that the stranger had already alerted the authorities, so she didn't dare leave to try to find food. All day they lay there.

Then, at dusk, a kindly Quaker farmer walked through the tall weeds near them—muttering, it seemed, to himself. But they could hear him say quietly, "My wagon stands in the barnyard of the next farm across the way. The horse is in the stable; the harness hangs on a nail." Then the man was gone. When the weary party arrived at the barnyard, not only was the wagon there, it was stocked with provisions![8]

Harriet Tubman was just one woman, but in the decade before the Civil War she made nineteen trips back and forth across the Mason-Dixon line to lead an estimated three hundred slaves to freedom. Believing her actions were inspired by God, she led so many to "the Promised Land" of freedom that she was nicknamed "Black Moses."[9]

God specializes in making up the difference. When we see God as he is—fully able—we will step out and influence—not in our power but God's. Does life have you lying facedown in a swamp, praying for deliverance? The idealist arrives in the same swamp as everyone else, but she believes God can deliver—she's banking on it! Look up; your provisions are waiting.

Living It Out
What did you learn about God in this chapter that released one of your fears?

In Israel, when God performed a memorable work, an altar was built, stone upon stone, that would help remind all who passed of God's great work. Make your own "altar" that will remind you of who God really is and who you really are. Now is a good time to let your leadership style soar. Make or buy something that reflects the *you* God made you to be. Put the "altar" where you will be able to see it daily, as a tangible reminder that *God is for you!*

Here are some altar ideas:

☐ a poem, song or story
☐ a quilt, cross-stitch or calligraphy
☐ a painting, water color or sculpture
☐ a photo, poster or Bible cover
☐ a plant, flower or tree
☐ a plaque, plate or pottery
☐ a key chain, locket or ring
☐ a bookmark, bookend or video
☐ a memorialized donation or scholarship fund
☐ a screen saver or screen frame for your personal computer

Chapter 5

A Woman
of Influence
Is Interdependent

IT WAS A SUNNY DAY. THE AIR WAS HOT AND THE WATER INVITING. A TEENAGE girl dove into the lake and almost never came up again. She was pulled to safety and rushed to the hospital—only to be told she would never walk again. In 1967, Joni Eareckson was a vibrant teen who dove into water too shallow and paid a high price. She was left a quadriplegic. But she clung to God in her pain, and he gave her the will to find other gifts and talents buried deep within.

Many people encouraged and challenged Joni along her road to recovery. She became adept at painting with a brush in her mouth. She learned to sing when no one thought she had anything to sing about. More than anything, Joni was given the ability to speak and write with hope and compassion. She is dependent on many people for her simplest needs, yet hundreds of others depend on her for encouragement and strength.

Her marriage to Ken Tada gives couples of all abilities encouragement. Her inspirational paintings hang in galleries and homes. Her books are bestsellers, and her voice is heard on radios across the country. She has a gift of leadership that created an international ministry called JF ("Joni and Friends"), seeking to meet the needs of the disabled and their families. In 1987 President Reagan named Joni to a national council on disability, and she serves on the boards of several major Christian ministries, including the National Religious Broadcasters Association. She says, "If I want the Lord Jesus to be glorified in my life, I must run the race not to please myself, but to please the Lord—and that often will mean taking time to stop and put my arm around a weaker friend."[1]

Though I have never met Joni, I was at one time one of those weaker friends, and the words she penned gave me wings to fly again. During a time when I was battling depression, I read one of her devotional books. Day after day, she challenged me deeper into God's Word—and there I found secret strength.

There are some verses in the Bible that say, "Two are better than one . . . if one falls down, his friend can help him up. . . . Though one may be overpowered, two can defend themselves. A cord of three strands is not quickly broken" (Eccles 4:9-10, 12). It's true, no one is an island. Relationships are some of life's greatest blessings and some of life's greatest pains. How are we supposed to relate to one another?

Finding Healthy Friendships

When we are overly dependent on our friends, we run the risk of quenching our obedience to God. We can also develop bad friendship patterns that isolate us from future relationships that could be a joy and blessing. On the other hand, relationships are essential for our well-being. We need to learn the difference between healthy interdependence and destructive dependence.

Interdependence says, "I'll be there for you." Dependence says, "You can't do it without me."

Interdependence says, "I want you to change and grow." Dependence says, "I want you to stay the same. Stay the same as me."

Interdependence says, "If opening up our friendship is healthy—let's do it." Dependence says, "No one else can be your friend."

Interdependence says, "I'll wait until it's convenient." Dependence says, "I'll impose on you, but you'll understand; after all, you love me, don't you?"

Interdependence says, "What can I do to help you?" Dependence says, "What can you do to help me?"

Interdependence says, "I'm grateful for what you've given." Dependence says, "You owe me more."

The Bible lists many principles for how we should relate to one another. Women of influence who work on these principles as the framework for their dealings with people will be far ahead, because the principles personalize the character of God to others.

Greet One Another

Because we moved so much during my childhood, my dear mom forced me to be the unofficial greeter wherever we went. I hated it at the time, but I am grateful now for her persistent prodding. Meeting new people is really hard for most women. It feels so risky—so vulnerable. It doesn't have to.

The most important aspect of greeting is to think of the other person first. Set yourself aside. When you think of the other person, you don't have time to think of yourself. If you struggle with meeting new people and making small talk, or if you feel awkward in social settings, ask someone who is good at it to share how she does it. Ask if you can tag along with her in the next social setting and learn the ropes. The best way to learn to meet new people is to meet many new people!

Build One Another Up

"Encourage one another and build each other up" (1 Thess 5:11). Words are a powerful tool. Words can build up and unleash potential or words can tear down and destroy.

One summer I spent every quiet time studying the words *mouth, words, tongue* and *gossip* in the Bible. Was I enlightened! All I wanted to find was a simple definition of what gossip was, so I could avoid it. My working definition of gossip came in the form of questions that I asked myself before I spoke:

Would I say this if the person was sitting here next to me?

Do I have permission to share this?

Can the person I tell this to do anything about the situation?

If the answer wasn't yes to all three, I kept my mouth shut! Even good news shared can backfire. Once, a friend joyously called me with the good news of a pregnancy. I jumped on the phone and called several friends who I knew would be so excited for her. Little did I know she was trying to call them to tell them herself. When she got through and they all responded with, "I know! Pam told me!" she called and confronted me. She quietly but firmly explained that she was hurt because I had robbed her of the joy of telling her friends and getting their surprised reactions. Now, even when someone shares good news, I try to ask if I should share it with others or wait until she has broken the news.

In a town near my own, a teenager sued a school district over a rumor started about him by a coach. The rumor spread throughout the staff and then on to the student body. It got to the point where the student was receiving over thirty phone calls a night from people seeking to confirm or dispel the rumor. He became so depressed at his destroyed reputation that he refused to get off the couch and had to be put on antidepressants.

When someone comes to me with some tasty gossip, I try to nip it in the bud as soon as possible. My favorite tactics include changing the subject, politely explaining that I don't think I need to know the information, or recommending that the bearer of the news allow the person to tell me directly. Sometimes, if I am alone with the gossiper, I'll explain that I think the topic would be gossip so it would be better left unsaid. For a direct confrontation I want to be alone, so I won't be embarrassing the other person in front of others or adding to the gossip cycle.

Admonish One Another

Gossip is the kissin' cousin to criticism. Criticism can seek and destroy in much the same way. It is crucial that women of influence learn the difference between admonishment and criticism. Admonishment is advice, instruction or warning. The goal of admonishment is to build up, strengthen or equip the person being admonished. The first key to successful admonishment is earning the right to say it. Too many people think that admonishment is a spiritual gift—wrong! Admonishment should be accompanied by a spiritual commitment of some kind. If you are going to point out a weakness in someone's life, you'd better be ready to offer to do something to help in that area, or you shouldn't say it!

The second key to successful admonishment is gentle wording. Galatians 6:1 reminds us to restore gently. And I like Colossians 4:6, which tells me to season my words with grace. Some women are so good at this kind of admonition that you go away feeling cared for and loved rather than ripped to shreds. That should be the result of godly admonishment. The hearer of the admonishment may feel a little introspective, because the Holy Spirit is at work, but she should also feel that the words were said because you truly care for her best interests. If you want to admonish for any other reason—keep quiet!

I try hard to correct others in the way I'd like to be corrected, and I try not to read criticism in where it isn't intended.

Still, at times criticism does hit the bull's-eye. At those times, I have to take the remarks to the feet of Jesus and ask him to sort through them. The Word tells us to throw down vain speculations, and I know Satan is the king of liars, so I'll want to reject the ones that come from him. But if there is even a granule of admonition from God, I want my heart to receive it.

This sorting process is never easy. Because criticism leaves one feeling so vulnerable, I have learned not to try to defend myself but rather to say, "Thank you for sharing your heart." Then I go before the Lord with my heavy heart. After I have spent time with Jesus over the content of the criticism, I'll pray over my response to it.

Be at Peace with One Another

I have several choices.

☐ I can forgive and go on without a word. This is often my method with the continually contentious critic. Responding to criticism from some people simply fuels more criticism, because what they want is either control or attention. Also, much of what hurts us is small, and I prefer to give others the benefit of the doubt and forgive, assuming they weren't intentionally seeking to hurt me.

☐ I can forgive and set an appointment for further discussion, clarification and admonishment. I'll want to respond to a critic who is young in the Lord because it is a good teaching opportunity (even if it is just to model for them the biblical way to admonish!). I need to respond if the person and I need to be reunited for fellowship or work. Philippians 2:2 tells me to be of one mind and heart with other believers. I also will want to respond in some appropriate way if the criticism was from a leader or supervisor. My response may be to follow the designated correction or to set up a conference to clarify my stand and bargain for a resolution.

☐ I can call in a mediator. If I am fearful of my confronter, I may want to request a meeting with a neutral third party who can help us iron out our differences.

Before any confrontation, I seek to set up as many guidelines as possible. Whose issue is this? Yours, mine, both, others'? Who needs to be at the meeting? Where shall we meet? How long shall we meet? It's important to avoid any further misunderstanding by trying to clarify the meeting parameters. I suggest that you pray through and set up some parameters, then offer these guidelines to the critic. This can help alleviate a dispute over the meeting. If you can't agree, ask for a mediator to arrange these as well.

Be determined to either resolve or forgive. Whatever you do, don't allow the criticism to sidetrack you from God's plan for you. If you are a woman of influence, expect criticism. It goes with the role. There are women who *do*, women who *follow* and women who *complain* about those who do and follow. If you are on the front lines in a battle, you take the hits. Those resting comfortably back in the barracks aren't on the firing line as you are. When you are a woman of influence, you will make things happen. And in making things happen, you stir up the status quo. And in stirring up the status quo, some people's comfort zones get shaken and they'll respond with criticism.

One day a letter landed on my desk. A long letter, full of attacks on my character, my motives, my ministry and my family. Usually I can deal quickly with criticism, but this was such a personal attack. It followed a long stretch of exhausting work and ministry, so I was very vulnerable to discouragement. As I read the letter, a dark cloud covered my heart. I cried out to God in my hurt. Then I got angry. Then I cried. Then I got depressed. I felt as if I were having an emotional knock-down, drag-out fight.

Satan wanted me so discouraged that I couldn't minister. And believe me, my flesh felt like giving in. I knew I could choose a bitter place or a broken place. It's natural to want to turn bitter. It's better to be broken over a hurt and allow God to heal it.

It took several months, but gradually my perspective returned. In my brokenness, I continued to do what God had called me to do. As I placed my eyes on Jesus and the needy world around me, a new, bolder resolve fortified my character. Whether your criticism happens at work, in ministry, in volunteer work or in the home, keep your eyes on God, his opinion and his plan. Healing happens as you continue in your passion.

Forgive One Another

Forgiveness is strategic to an ongoing healthy relationship. Forgiveness doesn't mean just forgetting that a wrong was done, sweeping the issue under the carpet. Forgiveness doesn't say, "Oh, that's okay," because a wrong inflicted is not okay!

Forgiveness is a decision of my will to stop the effect that an injustice done to me has on the development of my character. To help people understand forgiveness, my husband, Bill, created a set of six statements that we use in our speaking and counseling ministry.

Forgiveness says:

1. I forgive _____ (person) for _____ (offense).
2. I admit that what was done was wrong.
3. I do not expect _____ (person) to make up for what he (she) has done.
4. I will not use this offense to define who _____ (person) is.
5. I will not manipulate _____ (person) with the offense.
6. I will not allow the offense to stop my growth.

This is what Christ did for us. He didn't dismiss our sin; he said it was wrong. He didn't rationalize it or whitewash it. He died for it! Jesus didn't expect us to make up for our imperfection. That would be impossible. Once a sin is committed, it can't be uncommitted. We can go on to live out a healthy life and set up godly patterns, but we cannot undo what was done.

Jesus doesn't define us by our sin. When we come to him, we are made new creations and God sees us clothed in Christ's righteousness. Jesus doesn't manipulate us with our sin. He doesn't hang it over our head or stab us in the back with it. He gives us a clean slate. He frees us to grow into all he designed us to be. Forgiveness isn't a feeling; it is an action born out of a choice to love.

Get Along with One Another

The Bible tells us to bear with, live in harmony with, accept and have compassion on one another. We need to get along. The key principle in choosing to get along is found in Ephesians 4:2: "Be completely humble and gentle; be patient, bearing with one another in love." In 1 Peter 5:5 we are reminded to clothe ourselves in humility. A humble heart doesn't have to always be right. A humble heart doesn't care that anyone gets the glory—except God. A humble heart is not easily offended. A humble heart has learned that the secret to great leadership is servanthood. A humble heart seeks the greatest good of all. A humble heart can lovingly agree to disagree. A humble heart forgives readily; it doesn't sweat the small stuff. A humble heart majors on the majors and minors on the minors.

A top-ranking British official once entertained a haughty and sophisticated lady in his home. By mistake, the host's assistant asked her to sit on the left of her host rather than at the place of honor at his right. The visitor was offended and became indignant. Turning to the general, who was her host, she said, "I suppose you have real difficulty in getting your aide-de-camp to seat guests properly at the table."

"Oh, not at all," replied the general. "I have found that those that matter don't mind, and those that mind don't matter."[2]

Be Stretcher-Bearer Friends

We all need them, and we need to *be* them for others: "stretcher-bearers" are the handful of people you would call if something awful happened in your life. You *know* you can depend on them. When someone is injured in a battle, the wounded individual is loaded onto a stretcher and carried to help.

Luke tells the story of a man who was carried and then lowered through a roof so Jesus could help him. Seeing their faith—the faith of the friends—Jesus healed the man.

Who could you call if something happened to you, your husband, your child or your parents? Which friends would offer the kind of wisdom, consolation and support that you'd need? You need a committed handful of stretcher-bearer friends you can call when you are really hurting.

Often these friendships are built over time. When you've had long heart-to-heart conversations, calling when you are hurting seems natural. These friends have probably also seen you at your worst. They know your shortcomings and accept you anyway. All of the friends whom I would call in case of emergencies are friends to whom I've had to say "I'm sorry." These friends know I don't have it all together. I'm on a journey, just as they are. They are committed to seeing I stay on track until I arrive at the finish line.

These kind of relationships are rare. My stretcher-bearer friends are worth sacrificing to keep in touch with. I live far away from several of them, but I go out of my way, a few times a year, to spend time with these women.

One of my stretcher-bearer friends, Mary, calls just to keep in touch. We may not talk for months—but then we pick up exactly where we left off. When I was going through a rough time in ministry, I could call Mary, and she'd make time to listen. Once my car broke down at her house and my overnight stay turned into a several-day residency. She took the change in stride, because our relationship was important to her. She is important enough for me to sacrifice for also. You know who these friends are, because you don't screen calls from them!

I know I can't be this kind of friend to everyone, so I pray about which women around me I can serve in this way, and then I plan some time to keep in touch with them—ready to just listen or to answer an emergency call.

Accept One Another

We need to have realistic expectations of ourselves and others. Acceptance is embracing a person as a whole package. Sure, there are flaws, and many of those flaws need changing, but you'll never be an influence if the person feels loved conditionally. If people have to perform to win our acceptance, they will soon tire of the game and move away from us.

I was meeting with a woman I discipled. I sat and explained the next step that I thought she should take in her growth as a leader. I was rattling off names of young women she might challenge to a discipleship program. With every name, I'd get, "Pam, I don't think I can do this." And I would respond with a pep talk. Eventually, this quiet woman looked me straight in the eye and said with as much resolve as she could, "You're not listening to me! I'm saying I can't do that right now!"

Then I finally heard her. She was not philosophically opposed to any of the plan. In fact, someday she wanted to reproduce herself in others. She'd been trying to explain an inner conflict she'd been struggling with, and I was downplaying it. I had always been her cheerleader. She had always been able to look to me for acceptance and support, but now, when she really needed me, I was dumping unreal expectations on her. Fortunately she called me on it! I was pushing my agenda for her, rather than supporting the agenda God had for her. I apologized, backed off and listened.

It is very important to lead, encourage and lay out a vision for others, but the bottom line is acceptance. You have to help them get to God's place for them, not your place for them. Sometimes it is the same place; sometimes it is not. God is the best one to help your friend find his will for her own life. Your job is to help her stay plugged in to God. Her job is to listen to God.

Instruct One Another

Teaching is the basis for future leadership. How can we hold anyone to any standard that has not been clearly defined? How can we expect a job to be done if the person doing it has never been trained? How can we discipline or correct if we've never encouraged? A woman of influence desires to share where she has been so others can be equipped to get to God's destination. As is often said, "Give a man a fish and he can eat for a day; teach a man to fish and he can eat for a lifetime."

A women of influence is an enabler. She doesn't hoard knowledge; she shares knowledge, hoping others will succeed. Much insight and encouragement can be gained by those who have gone before.

Elisabeth Elliot, in her biography of Amy Carmichael, *A Chance to Die,* writes of her response to Amy's life:

Amy Carmichael became for me what some now call a role model. She was far more than that. She was my spiritual mother. She showed me the shape of godliness. For a time, I suppose, I thought she must have been perfect, and that was good enough for me. As I grew up I knew she could not have been perfect, and that was better, for it meant that I might possibly walk in her footprints. If we demand perfect role models we will have, except for the Son of Man himself, none at all.[3]

Be Hospitable to One Another

Our homes should be an extension of our influence. Too many homes today feel as if they have a moat, drawbridge and armed soldiers guarding the entrance. Our society is so mobile that we don't know our neighbors—or even try to. We commute to work, and the last thing we want to do when we get home is entertain.

That's the fallacy: Hospitality is not entertaining. Hospitality is an attitude of opening up your life so that others can come in. There are three fears to overcome in order to be a hospitable person: (1) I don't have enough time, (2) I don't have enough money, (3) I don't have enough space. The major problem with all three statements is that they begin with *I*. Hospitality begins with *You*.

No time. No one ever has enough time; that's why a hospitable person learns to party as she goes. If it is important to you, you'll be able to creatively carve out time. Take snacks with you for the car pool. Grab a pile of magazines, tie them with a bow and drop them off to a friend. Get two mochas on the way to work and chat with a coworker for a few minutes. Keep a "party box" supplied with crepe paper streamers, balloons, tape, posterboard and markers; you can use these at short notice to help celebrate somebody.

No money. The best party I ever gave was a birthday celebration for Bill while we were in seminary. We were broke, and so were all of our seminary friends. I sent out invitations written on brown paper lunch bags. The recipients were asked to fill the bag with their favorite snacks: that would be their gift to Bill. At the party, I threw out a bunch of art supplies, tape and scissors, and each person was asked to create a gift for Bill out of another brown lunch bag. The gifts were a riot. He got bags for under his eyes, a brown paper briefcase, brown paper sunglasses, a brown paper suit. I provided the drinks and popcorn. I'm sure the entire party cost well under ten dollars—maybe under five!

No space. Many of us avoid hospitality because we feel a pressure to have a perfect home. The time required to make it perfect may seem too great, or we may feel our home is not nice enough for our guests. My mom used to tell me, "People are coming to see us, not the house."

But if your tiny dorm room or apartment is not large enough, or your home is too small for an event, just move the party! Go to the park, the beach, the lake, the garage, the yard, the driveway, the community center or the barn! One creative couple I knew lived in a tiny studio apartment, so they would offer to cook elaborate meals and take them to the homes of their friends. All their friends loved it, because they lived hectic dual-career lives and seldom got a home-cooked meal!

Redefining Relationships

There are "friends of the heart and friends for the road."[4] Relationships will change. It is how we handle the change that is important. Some friendships are for a season. I have discovered that my relationships need to be defined each time there is a significant change in life. One of us may move, get a new job, have a baby or whatever. I have found redefinition of a friendship a growing experience for both of us if the friendship had a definition to begin with. When you are honest in relationships, your friends will be freed to respond with known expectations, rather than tied in knots wondering where they stand with you. I continually weigh before the Lord which women I need to spend time with. Knowing the purpose for the relationship often helps me evaluate whether it is a permanent or temporary one.

Sometimes people want more from you than you can give, or more than you feel God wants you to give. It is better to be honest and tactfully explain your limitations than to promise something you have no intention of following through on (or that you're not sure you will follow through on). I ask someone to explain where she sees the relationship going from this point, and I share my viewpoint as well. The amount of time you spend redefining will depend on the time you have available and how much time you and God have invested in that relationship.

Sometimes people step out of my life and it has nothing to do with me. If the person has been a close friend, a colleague or a disciple, I try to find out if she is struggling with a personal or spiritual problem. For some women, I can only drop a quick note in the mail or leave a brief message on voice mail. But if I can, I try to have a face-to-face redefinition. I always try to be loving and upbeat and to really listen. I try not to burn any bridges that I might need to walk back over.

As you redefine, review how God called your friendship into existence. Focus on the special needs that the friendship addressed for the season. Elaborate the positive qualities that each of you brought to the relationship at the time. This is especially important in a dating relationship, because you want to leave the person free to date again, not so wounded that it takes years to recover. In a friendship with another believer, focus on God's sovereignty and care.

When redefining a relationship with an unbeliever or in a secular work setting, drop all the Christian lingo. Refrain from telling people God called you to leave them. They may not understand the "calling" aspect of a personal relationship with God. They could interpret it as some weird channeling experience or take it to mean that God doesn't like them. Your relationship may have to change, but try to keep the door open for their connection to God.

Serve One Another

The servant's attitude is a hard one to master. It goes against everything we've been taught in the concrete jungle. We're supposed to look out for number one, go for the jugular. We don't get a lot of praise for serving. True servanthood grows from a humble heart. A servant's heart sees a need and seeks to meet that need without personal gain. But being a servant is tough, because we fight the feeling of being taken advantage of.

Servanthood became very real to me when my oldest was four years old. It was Easter morning and it was raining. I got my two toddlers ready for this special day and then went to get dressed myself. I came out of my bedroom and found the two boys stomping in mud puddles on the patio. I called them in, but Zach was reluctant, so I went out in the rain after him. He reached up for me to carry him and promptly marched his muddy feet up my new white skirt.

I cried out, "Zach, please stop!"

"Why?" asked Zach.

"This skirt is special. Mommy is a person too!"

Then Brock chimed in, "You're not a person—you're a mommy!"

Colleen Townsend Evans says the best way to test your servant spirit is to notice how you react when you are treated like a servant. My servant's heart wasn't too healthy that day!

Servanthood is necessary for accomplishing goals as a team. Sometimes we have to roll up our sleeves and do what needs to be done, even if it is not our position, our calling or our gift. Sometimes things need doing and you, God's servant, need to do them! The best leaders are first the best servants. We have to know how to follow well in order to know how to lead well. Jesus said, "Whoever wants to be first must be last of all and servant of all" (Mk 9:35 NRSV).

For You—Not Me

One day I was complaining to God about all the chairs Bill and I set up, the coffeepots we clean, the vacuuming, the errands—the servant's work. I was trying to explain to God that he was wasting all our experience and education by having us have do so much menial work. That afternoon, Bill was to perform a small wedding for a young couple.

During the ceremony, the bride, who had no bridesmaids, became entangled in the candelabra, and her train caught as she turned to light the unity candle. Bill, who was already holding her flowers, saw the bride's need. He knew she needed to be presented at her best because this was her special day. Bill gently bent down and straightened the hem of her dress.

I started to cry. *That's why I married Bill, Father. He is such a servant. He never tires of meeting the lowest needs. He bends down to serve your bride, the church. I need to be more like him—more like you! For you, Lord, for others—not for me!*

Living It Out

It is healthy to have a variety of relationships. Are you balanced, or do you need to deepen a few relationships or make new ones? Are all your friends non-Christians or all Christians? Choose one of these friendship-building activities:

1. Personally thank those you think of as your stretcher-bearers.

2. Schedule time with a person with whom you'd like a deeper friendship.

3. Make a list of places you can meet new friends. Meet someone new this week.

4. Redefine a relationship by meeting with that person.

Chapter 6

A Woman
of Influence
Takes Initiative

N O!" THE WOMAN SHOUTED, ALMOST INSTINCTIVELY, AS SHE ROSE TO
her feet. The sound echoed through the meeting hall.

An assembly of delegates had just vetoed her husband's request to be employed as an itinerant pastor for the movement. She was shocked. She was so sure this was God's will for her and her husband.

She was, at first, filled with deep frustration at what appeared to be a serious roadblock keeping them from their dream. But she was then struck with the realization that this was God's permission for them to fly. God had other plans, bigger plans for them.

The couple, sensing this was God's way of leading, joined hands and left the building. Catherine and William Booth walked away from an opportunity to minister in one location, earn a somewhat secure income and keep the successful ministry they already had achieved.

But they felt a call to minister to all of England, especially the poorest and most downtrodden. Catherine disliked indecision. She felt life was too short to wait around. Catherine looked for ways to make a difference—and if she didn't find any, she created them. That day, the Booths left the known and stepped into the unknown to launch a ministry that would become the Salvation Army.

Years later Catherine captured her heart as she penned a letter to one of her children. "We are made for larger ends than earth can compass. Oh let us be true to our exalted destiny."[1]

She had been a sickly and fragile child, unable to attend traditional school for most of her life. Instead of wasting her time feeling sorry for herself, she flooded her mind with great literature. By the time she was twelve, she had read the Bible eight times, and she loved the classics—everything from Dickens to Dante.

She married the bright and articulate though poorly educated William Booth, and they launched into a life characterized by faith, risk and servanthood. Catherine didn't wait to be invited to speak. One day, after William had preached, she asked if she might say a few words. William consented, and the result was a stirring sermon which moved the hearts of the congregation for a second time that morning. It also removed a barrier. It was unusual for women to speak publicly in England at this time, but news of Catherine's inspirational gift spread, and soon she was asked to speak quite frequently. Catherine was as talented in the pulpit as was her itinerant preacher husband. Both drew huge crowds throughout England.

Catherine Booth was a dedicated mother who raised eight children. She didn't wait for her children to grow up before she ministered. She took them to do ministry with her. All eight went on to leadership positions within the Salvation Army.

She felt that much of what society wanted women to do was a waste of their time and talents. She was frustrated by the emphasis on the material, external frivolousness of her world. "It will be a happy day for England, when Christian ladies transfer their attention from poodles and terriers to destitute and starving children."[2] Under Catherine's leadership, many women did just that!

She threw herself into a political battle later in her life when she became aware of the selling of young women for prostitution. In England there was no penalty for pimping girls. If the girl was younger than thirteen, she was too young to testify. If she was over thirteen, she was at the age of consent, and all girls were treated as if they had consented!

Catherine appealed to the Queen. After several years of trying to raise the awareness of the public, she saw a new law passed that raised the age of consent to eighteen. The law made it a criminal offense to seduce or procure women for immoral purposes, gave authorities searching rights, and made men and women equal under the law because it was equally criminal to solicit men or women. When Catherine passed away, fifty thousand mourners filed past to pay respects to a woman who had helped a generation believe God for a better life.

I'm Ready
Once we discover our passion and have a proper view of God and ourselves, we are ready for action. We too are ready to initiate change in our world and make a difference.

A woman of initiative knows where she's going and is excited about taking others with her. Initiative is where the rubber meets the road. Vision without initiative is like a heart that doesn't beat. Passion without particulars is just emotion. Passion will lay the foundation, but it is initiative that will lay the bricks, build the walls and finish off the house where hope can live.

How Can I Decide?
In Proverbs 3:5-6 God says, "Trust in the LORD with all your heart and

lean not on your own understanding; in all your ways acknowledge him, and he will make your paths straight."

And in Psalm 37:4-6 he says, "Delight yourself in the LORD and he will give you the desires of your heart. Commit your way to the LORD; trust in him and he will do this: he will make your righteousness shine like the dawn, the justice of your cause like the noonday sun."

Proverbs 16:3 says, "Commit your work to the LORD, and your plans will be established" (NRSV).

Proverbs 16:9 teaches, "The human mind plans the way, but the LORD directs the steps" (NRSV).

The promises are there. If I trust and commit my plans to God, he'll make the path straight before me. If I delight in God, he'll give me the desires of my heart.

If you do first that which you know to be God's will from the Bible, then you are abiding in God, and he will ensure that you stay in his plan as long as you have a yielded heart. If you do the known, he'll lead through the unknown.

But how do I trust? How do I commit myself to him? What steps can I take to initiate God's will in my life?

Step Up
To be a woman of influence, you must have goals. But goals don't have to be intimidating. Are you freaked out each time you climb a flight of stairs? Of course not! Goals are simply a set of steps. One after another, these steps will get you from where you are now to where you want to be.

A stairway model is best used in conjunction with a brainstorming list. Let's say you are right now the mother of two preschoolers, ages four and three. In two years, both children will be in school, at least from 8 a.m. to 1 p.m. You have two years of college out of the way and you have dreams of finishing your degree and running your own business. You pray with your family and decide a home-based business would provide the income your family needs and eventually give you the flexibility to return to school and finish your education. Brainstorm and list what you may need to do to get a business off the ground. Some of these steps may be on your list:

☐ pray with family
☐ talk to professionals in the field I'd like to work in
☐ go to a business fair
☐ make connections in SCORE (retired business professionals)
☐ contact Chamber of Commerce for information on laws (many have new business packets)
☐ check out home business books from the library
☐ check out home business information and newsletters (maybe on the Internet)
☐ obtain financial information
☐ make a business plan
☐ secure financing and supplies
☐ set up work space
☐ plan advertising or public relations

Next, arrange the steps in logical order, putting the beginning steps at the bottom of the stairway. For example, you may want to research the job field and talk to professionals early, because that market may be sluggish or a new development may have occurred. After you have each step plugged into the chart, go back to each step and place a target date next to the step. Now, before you lies the framework for achieving your goal. Your goal staircase might look like this:

September: Launch business.

August: Create a business plan, secure capital/resources.

July: Narrow choices and investigate details.

June: Contact Chamber of Commerce and SCORE; investigate financial leads.

May: Attend business fair; talk to others in business area of interest.

April: Pray with family; determine budget and financial need; network with other women in business; read books, newsletters, magazines and journals.

Your Plan!

What is the challenge in your life? Are you a student? Newly married? Planning a wedding? Setting goals for your children or your marriage? Is a job change or career reentry ahead? Are you looking toward an empty nest or retirement? Do you have dreams waiting to be fulfilled?

Think of one dream that you have. Now brainstorm a list of things that would have to happen in order to achieve that dream.

Take that list and plug the ideas into a stairstep diagram such as the one below:

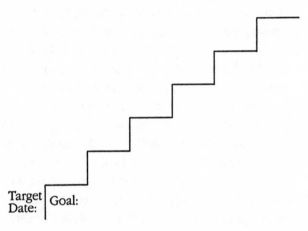

Target
Date: Goal:

You now have a workable plan for achieving that dream. Goals are just dreams with deadlines.[3]

Look Within

In order to maintain a balanced life, it is helpful to write goals in four major life areas—goals that will help you take another *step* forward. You'll want to develop your STEP plan as follows.

☐ Spiritual life

☐ Team

☐ Energy

☐ Productivity

S: your spiritual life. In this area you will want to write goals concerning your relationship with God. Areas to consider are your prayer life, Bible study, quiet time, Scripture memorization, church attendance, fasting, corporate worship, small group connections and so on.

The key to a rich spiritual life is to consistently "be filled with the Spirit" (Eph 5:18). When a woman is filled with the Holy Spirit, it means that she is yielding to God's rule in her life. You and God are walking along in fellowship. Every moral decision in life is like a fork in the road. God points at one of the choices and says, "That's sin." At that point you can simply agree with God, deal with the problem and keep walking in fellowship, or you can say, "No, God, I don't agree," and choose to travel down that sinful path. At any time, on that path, you can stop, agree with God by confessing that your actions and attitudes were wrong and return to walking in fellowship.

When you walk in the power of the Spirit, you will avoid the problems that are created by your own wrongdoing. We live in a fallen world, so there will be hassles. But God tells us in 1 Peter 3:17, "It is better, if it is God's will, to suffer for doing good than for doing evil." I used to struggle with asking people to make courageous changes in their lives because it meant they would have to walk a sometimes hard road of growth and redefining of life according to God's Word. But then I realized that everyone in life is already walking a hard road. Either we choose to do wrong and suffer the consequences of sin or we choose to do right and push through the pains of growth.

I have a dear friend, Marjorie, who has endured abandonment by a husband, the death of her only son, the loss of a career position shortly before retirement and a home that burned nearly to the ground. Her ability to bounce back after such severe trauma has amazed me

Right after the fire, I had the privilege of taking Marjorie shopping for a few toiletries and necessities she wanted for the next day. We gathered the items and stood in line. We looked disheveled and downcast. The checker said, "Cheer up, ladies, it can't be that bad."

Answering for Marjorie, I said, "Oh, it could."

"Now ladies, it's close to Christmas, cheer up. Life can't be this bad."

Knowing I had to rescue this kind man, I said, "My friend's house burned to the ground today."

"Oh, I guess it *can* be that bad!" He continued checking the items, then kindly reached across the counter to my friend and said, "I'm so sorry for your loss. I'll pray for you."

On the way to the parking lot, Marjorie turned to me and said, "Pam, the Bible says in the end it'll all burn anyway; mine just went up a little sooner than yours." She smiled. As we hugged and laughed in the crisp Christmas air, I realized I was standing in the presence of a woman whose spiritual life was vibrant.

Marjorie believes we are actually supposed to "give thanks in all circumstances, for this is God's will for you in Christ Jesus" (1 Thess 5:18). As a result, she has a reserve of strength to rely on. Bitterness, anger and resentment take a toll on your heart, and they disconnect you from God's supernatural power source. Frustration, anxiety and depression also eat up valuable time. In my years of ministering to women, I have noticed that the women who maintain a positive outlook can carry much more responsibility and achieve many more goals. Write down some goals that have the purpose of keeping your heart connected and yielded to God.

T: your team. This area includes goals that affect the "team" of people close to you: your spouse, children, parents, friends, a dating relationship and so on. Goals for relationships must be either mutually agreed on ("My husband and I will go out on a date each Thursday") or personally decided on ("I will send a special card in each of my children's lunches once a week").

You can only achieve goals over which you have a degree of control. For instance, you may desire to have a happier marriage and think the quickest way to achieve that is to fix your husband. The problem is, you have no control over your husband. You have the ability to change only yourself and must trust God to work with your mate.

You may have a goal of becoming closer friends with someone. It's a good goal as long as you realize you cannot control the friend's involvement in your relationship. You can carve out time to spend with a friend and decide to be encouraging to her, but you can't dictate her response.

It is especially important in your private life to guard your sexual purity, whether you are single or married. You can wipe out years of influence with one indiscretion. In my years in ministry, I have seen women go from the pinnacle of influence and success to the pit of ridicule and rebellion because they didn't guard their hearts.

First Thessalonians 4:3 is clear when it says it is God's will that we should avoid sexual immorality. Immorality is sex that is outside the context of marriage. Premarital sex, homosexuality and adultery are not options for the woman of influence. The guidelines should be drawn prior to marriage so that your purity and the purity of your dating partner are maintained. If the sexual encounter is looked at as a continuum, with holding hands on one end and sexual intercourse on the other, your personal line of holiness should be drawn at a point where your heart, mind and body will remain pure.

Each woman needs to define her own boundaries before entering a relationship. Sharing these boundaries with a friend or mentor will help you remain true to your own convictions. These convictions should be discussed early in a dating relationship.

If you are married, your mentor and close friends should be encouraged to ask you about your thought life, your romantic relationship, and about your feelings toward your husband. The uniqueness and privacy of the marriage should be protected, but accountability in this vital area is helpful.

This is also the time to write goals concerning your mothering, your role as a daughter, an in-law, or any other relationship you'd like to see grow. It can even include lists of activities, romantic date ideas, birthdays—anything that will help promote close relationships.

E: your energy. Include here issues involving your personal well-being. This can include your physical health, your emotional development, hobbies or social needs. This area may also address goals ranging from wardrobe needs to counseling or support group assignments—whatever will help you be well enough or have enough energy to accomplish the goals you have set in the other areas of your life.

I like to recheck my priorities on a regular basis. Patrick Marley recommends that we arrange our priorities according to who will cry at our funeral.[4] Daisy Hepburn advises women, "Do first that which only *you* can do."[5] I know that I'm the only one who can exercise for me or read for me. I am also the only mother my boys will ever have. Only I can be my husband's wife and lover. Everything else has to follow after those. We have to take care of ourselves if we are to maintain our influence in the lives of others.

Sometimes the best thing you can do to take care of yourself is to "seize the moment." Some days where I live are just "beach days." I wake up, the sun is hot and bright and the ocean seems to beckon me. Often I'll throw the beach bag in the car with a few snacks and drinks and I'll pick up the kids from school and head straight to the beach for a few hours while everyone else is doing homework. Goals allow you to be spontaneous and guilt-free because you'll know when and where to jump back on track. There is time to stop and smell the roses or build a few sand castles!

P: your productivity. In this area, your goals can include career plans, education plans and ministry plans. Ministry plans will include personal areas of influence, such as discipleship or church leadership responsibilities, as well as any public ministry plans, such as being in charge of a ministry or running special events. If you are in management or own your own business, you may want to include a copy of your business plan too. Include any goals that will be competing for your time. You will be more productive day by day when you have a clear plan of action.

In college, I was on the springboard diving team and a student leader in Campus Crusade for Christ. During my first season, the two never conflicted. In fact, my ministry was furthered by my diving. By the end of the season, I had shared Christ with the entire women's team and most of the men's swim team. The challenge of diving also helped me overcome the barrier of fear. Sharing Jesus helped me overcome the fear of people, and getting back up and trying again after hitting the water—HARD—helped me hurdle the fear of failure.

However, during the second season, about half of the meets were moved from Fridays to Tuesdays. Tuesdays were leadership training, ministry planning and Bible study night for Crusade. The first Tuesday, I missed Bible study. The second Tuesday I came late. As I saw the next Tuesday coming up I knew I had to choose. I talked with the woman who was discipling me. I talked with the woman that had discipled her. I talked to a Christian coach. I talked to my friends and my parents. There was no consensus. After church on Sunday, I grabbed my Bible and went off to talk to God. The sermon had been in the book of 1 John so I decided to start there. I got stopped in my tracks in 1 John 2:15-17: "Do not love the world or anything in the world. If anyone loves the world, the love of the father is not in him. For everything in the world—the cravings of sinful man, the lust of his eyes and the boasting of what he has and does—comes not from the Father but from the world. The world and its desires pass away, but the man who does the will of God lives forever."

God made me take a long hard look at why I was diving. It wasn't to stay in shape. I had three PE classes and I was a gymnastics instructor.

It wasn't to share my faith. I'd already shared with everyone I could. I was diving for me. I'd come to enjoy the glory of winning and the delight of center stage. I liked the tan! I knew I was not good enough to get a diving scholarship to further my education. Diving was interfering with new challenges of ministry God was presenting to me. For me diving was now the wrong choice. I made personal appointments with all my coaches and explained my decision. Some took it well, some didn't. I talked to the members of my team and explained my decision to them and offered my continued support and friendship. In a very short time, I was put in leadership positions in ministry where I learned the foundational skills that are vital in my life today.

One of my role models for ministry has been Corrie ten Boom. Corrie was part of a dedicated Christian family that hid Jews during the Holocaust, and she spent years in a concentration camp for her love of the Jewish people. I am one generation away from being privileged to have heard her or met her. However, her writing has had a profound effect on me. One day while I was reading a devotional she wrote, a short, simple paragraph grabbed my attention:

When a house is on fire and you know that there are people in it, it is a sin to straighten pictures in that house. When the world about you is in great danger, works that are in themselves not sinful can become quite wrong.[6]

As you set goals for your own work and ministry, make this your prayer: *Lord, help me clarify my purpose by seeing the state of the world through your eyes.*

Look Ahead

Goals are our attempt to take the priorities God lays out in his Word and the twenty-four hours he gives us each day and make the best use of them. Goals are not rules! Goals are just guidelines to your dreams. The overarching aim in writing goals is to plan enough to accomplish the best of what God has planned for you, yet be flexible enough to change so that you accomplish the best of what God has for you. Even though I have goals, each day is held up to God with open hands and the prayer "Not my will but Thy will."

In order to effectively apply our dreams and desires we must fit them into the time frame of life. We must therefore strategically look ahead to the stages of life we are approaching.

Long-Term Goals

What are some of the life changes ahead on the road for you and your family in the next seven to ten years? Try to picture yourself in ten years—how old will you be? How old will your husband, or children or parents be? Their life stages will effect you. If you are single, what dreams would you like to see occur, even if you do not marry? What character traits would you like to develop? What wisdom, knowledge or training would you like to receive? What kind of person would you like to become? Weigh out your heart's desire before the Lord, then write some goals for the long term. Many goals cost money to achieve. Note in the margin with a $ any goals that cost; then, at the bottom of your goal sheet, add up the cost and note any additional financial goals that need to be added in order to finance the other goals. Here's an example:

Spiritual Life

By the time I am forty-five:

☐ I want to have read through the Bible five more times.

☐ I want to have completed all New Testament studies in my *NIV Quiet Time Bible* (IVP).

Short-Term Goals

After you've written your long-term goals, you'll want to take each long-term goal and write out specific steps you'll need to take in the next two to five years to accomplish those goals. Choose a consistent target date for all your goals (for example: by the time I am twenty, thirty, forty, fifty and so on). Now complete your list of short-term goals and the financial impact of each.

Example: Spiritual Life

By the time I am forty:

☐ I'd like to have read through the Bible using two unique versions: the *Inductive Study Bible* and the *NIV Quiet Time Bible*.

☐ I want to have completed the studies of the Gospels in my *NIV Quiet Time Bible*.

Yearly Goals

Each year, in late August, I write my goals for the upcoming year. Earlier in the summer, I write the goals for the women's ministry of our church and the ministry Bill and I run together. Summer is an emotional fresh start for me. For others, January is a fresh start. For my family, the school year has such a huge impact that prior to the opening of school we all reevaluate. At this evaluation time ask yourself: Am I chipping away at the goals that are most important to me? Is there anything I can delegate to someone else, to get it done better or more quickly? Can I eliminate one responsibility before I take on another? Complete your list of goals, remembering to note the financial implications. This is the time to be very specific!

Example: Spiritual Life

This year I will:

☐ use the *NIV Quiet Time Bible* for my devotions from September till May, starting in Genesis.

☐ do a study of Matthew in my *Inductive Study Bible* this summer.

You'll also want to get an organizer with a monthly calendar section in which to record important dates ahead of time. I write birthdays in a bright color and also note them at the bottom of the month before so I can buy gifts or cards in time. I keep a copy of my goals in my organizer for quick review and reminder. I also keep a copy of the boys' "Learner and Leader" goals for the year, as well as a sheet with

Bill's top priorities that affect me. My organizer goes everywhere with me, because I want to have needed information at my fingertips.

It is good to set up natural review times every few months to see how you are progressing. I usually use my anniversary, my birthday and one day of summer vacation as natural reevaluation times. At those times, I try to find time for longer quiet times with God, heart-to-heart talks with Bill and one-on-one time with the boys. I pencil in an average weekly schedule at this time as a visual aid to show whether I am overbooking my life. Bill and I compare schedules and make adjustments.

Writing out an average weekly schedule makes our most important goals a natural part of our life. For example: bedtime at our home is marked out in a one-hour block to include showers, Bible reading and devotions, family read-aloud of a classic in literature and time to chat with each child about his day. In order to attain the goals of family devotions and reading, we had to make those a regular part of our schedule.

Once a month, Bill and I set aside a morning to coordinate calendars and check up on the important goals. I come into this meeting with a list of questions and my ASAP list for that month.

Then each week we try for a breakfast or lunch date to touch base and coordinate our lives. These can get squeezed or interrupted, so in a pinch we grab twenty minutes and compare calendars—that's an imperative. Once a week, I do "To Do" lists for each day of the coming week. Each evening we do a five-minute preview of the next day, update changes and exchange new information. Each morning after my devotions, I run through my "To Do" list and reprioritize, delegate or drop things off my list.

If you use a weekly schedule, you can write at the top your focus for each day. You can note your husband's or children's priorities as well. At the bottom, write your daily imperative: If your day spins out of control, what one thing do you need to accomplish that day, even if you can't do anything else? For example, on Thursday, my imperative is finding some romantic time with Bill. On Saturday, it is cleaning the house—even if it is just the living room, kitchen and bath—because Sunday usually means company at our house.

Included at the end of this chapter is a budget worksheet, because finances that spin out of control will seriously impede your ability to reach your goals.[7]

If you will tenaciously apply these steps in your journey, you will initiate and achieve your goals. You will become a woman of initiative who really can get things done. God wants you to feel a sense of accomplishment. He knows you are a champion. God tells you, "Run in such a way that you may win" (1 Cor 9:24 NASB).

You and God can set a winning course. Hang on to those goals and dreams—even if no one else does! Remember:

☐ Walt Disney was once fired from a newspaper for lack of ideas.

☐ Thomas Edison's teachers said he was too stupid to learn anything.

☐ Albert Einstein's teacher once remarked that Albert was "mentally slow, unsociable and adrift forever in his foolish dreams."

☐ Leo Tolstoy, author of *War and Peace,* flunked out of college and was described as "unable and unwilling to learn."

☐ The father of world-famous sculptor François Rodin said, "I have an idiot for a son."

☐ Henry Ford went broke five times before he succeeded.

☐ Beethoven's teacher called him hopeless as a composer.

☐ Louisa May Alcott, author of *Little Women,* was encouraged by her family to try to find work as a servant or seamstress.[8]

Set a plan and stick to it. You can do it, with a little bit of initiative.

Living It Out

Write out your long-term, short-term and yearly goals. In pencil, mark out your average weekly schedule. Ask yourself these three questions:

1. Are these goals measurable?

2. Are they reachable with God's help?

3. Are my goals and priorities accurately reflected in my daily schedule?

Share what you have written with your spouse or a close friend or mentor, to see if he or she agrees with your answers.

Now look at how your finances add up and how well they reflect your goals. For the following worksheet, look back over the past twelve months and find an average monthly amount that you've been spending in each category.

Monthly Budget Worksheet

Income

    Salaries:

    Other:

Total income:

Expenses

    Tithe:

    Taxes:

    Housing (all expenses including rent or mortgage, insurance, upkeep, decorating, all utilities):

    Groceries:

    Auto (car payments, gas, upkeep, insurance, tax and license):

    Insurance (life, health and any other insurance):

    Debt (all debt excluding mortgage and monthly minimum payments):

    Entertainment/Recreation (eating out, tickets, video rental, any other activity, plus a monthly vacation savings amount):

    Work Expenses (childcare costs; any professional expenses):

    Clothing (list a monthly dollar figure for each family member):

    Savings/Retirement:

    Medical Expenses (any copayments, medical or dental bills not covered by insurance; monthly cost of prescriptions and over-the-counter medications):

Miscellaneous (personal care needs—haircuts, cosmetics, dry cleaning; personal allowance for each family member; unreimbursed ministry expenses; gifts; educational costs; hobbies; postage; photos; magazines and so on):

Total expenses:

Subtract expenses from income:

If income exceeds expenses, plan how to invest or give away the surplus. If expenses exceed income, plan some quick action to cut expenses, raise income or both.

Chapter 7

A Woman
of Influence
Has Integrity

THE WORDS JUST ROLLED OUT OF NATALIE'S MOUTH. HER BOSS WANTED her to use a business practice that Natalie thought was unethical. When the idea came up Natalie prayed, *God, help me—I need an answer now! I want all my life to glorify you.* Then the words sprang from her heart and into the conversation: "I just can't do that!"

The air was tense. Natalie knew she had to stand her ground, but she was concerned about being sensitive to those around her. *What if they don't understand? Am I being too tough? Am I saying this in a way that will glorify you, Lord?*

Natalie had rededicated her life to Christ a few years before, and she'd steadily grown in her relationship with Christ. She was a manager, so she felt a responsibility to the women who worked under her, some of whom were nonbelievers or young believers.

Sometimes Integrity Pays Off

"I stood my ground and refused to compromise," Natalie shared with excitement, "and my sales went up!" A few months later, she felt that perhaps God wanted her to cut back her work hours for the sake of her family and ministry priorities. She decided not to work on weekends, except during a few big marketing weeks. Her sales went up again! Then she was asked to be a support person in a counseling ministry. The commitment would tie her up every other Wednesday evening for several months. Wednesday nights were some of her big sales times. She felt God impressing her to take on the ministry. Her sales went up once again! Within weeks she was the top salesperson in the distributorship. She has stayed at the top since. Reflecting on the success, Natalie states emphatically, "I knew God would be there for me, if I was there for him."

Integrity pays. Integrity opens doors because people learn to trust you. In a survey of 2,600 managers, the managers were asked what constituted superior executive leadership. Topping the list was honesty.[1]

"I can only do it if it is honest." Natalie's words reverberated in Cathy's heart. Cathy was cutting corners in her business because she was panicked over providing for her family as a single mom. *God, this is a biggie! If I am dishonest, I feel I'm not trusting you and I want to trust you. But if I am honest, I feel I will be left behind in this competitive business!* Cathy hesitatingly resolved that night to run her business with integrity. Some weeks later she approached Natalie to give her a big hug and thank her for having the courage to do her job honestly. "My business has done better too! But the best part is that I have peace. And I have grown spiritually by leaps and bounds too!" Cathy's new goal is to give something back to someone else in the way God used Natalie to give to her.

Sometimes Integrity Costs

"Sandra, you can no longer help those people from your church with their financial needs. You are forbidden to give any financial advice outside the walls of this institution. It's a conflict of interest. Take your choice—it's this job or your volunteer work."

Being a woman who had gone through a huge financial turnaround due to a divorce, Sandra was sensitive to women who needed financial counseling. Most were widows on fixed incomes who couldn't afford to pay for financial advice or who were too overwhelmed with the new responsibility of managing an income. Sandra was asked by her pastor to help some of them. She volunteered to help others. She felt teaching women how to balance their accounts and how to understand different investment opportunities was the least she could do to help these women in such desperate straits.

She tried on several occasions to explain to her boss that she had crossed no legal boundaries and felt ethically obligated to help those less fortunate. After battling with the decision for many months, she quit the company. Her heart wasn't with money; it was with people. She held several part-time positions while praying that God would provide her with a full-time position where she could use her talents *and* help people.

Sandra waited and waited. It wasn't until several years later that she was approached by a company that specialized in the needs of the elderly. They needed someone who had her skills and a heart for the older generation. They approached Sandra because of her reputation for helping older women, a reputation gained by depriving herself for years.

A woman of influence seeks to weave character into her life ahead of time so that, when put in a pinch, she can decide the right thing to do on the spot. Integrity is a commitment to live consistently with what you know to be true about life.

What's Holiness, Anyway?

"So whether you eat or drink or whatever you do, do it all for the glory of God" (1 Cor 10:31). The woman of influence seeks to live all of her life so that others can see her good works and glorify her Father who is in heaven (Mt 5:16). She knows that good works don't buy her way into heaven. However, because she is heaven bound, freed from the judgment of sin, she can freely choose what is best. It's her desire to seek excellence, because it is her gift of love to the One who loved her enough to die for her.

Images of holiness often conjure up pictures of nuns' habits and a life cloistered away from the real world. But holiness isn't only for those inside the walls of a protected community; holiness is for everyone.

Integrity desires to be usable to God. So often we pray, *God, really use me,* but we don't want to go through the process of becoming usable. Let's say you came to my house for dinner and I offer you something to drink. I set before you two crystal glasses, beautifully etched, both containing the same sparkling water. However, one goblet has impurities floating in it—a dead fly, some dirt, a little leftover food. The water in the other goblet is sparkling clean. Which glass will you choose?

The sparkling clean one, I hope! It is the same with God. When he looks around to see who to use for the highly honorable task of representing him, he wants a pure container for the message to be delivered. If we have sin in our life that we refuse to deal with, or if we have specifically disobeyed God's will for us, we are like the impure glass. If we seek to be influential but are sloppy about obeying God in our personal lives, then the message will be distorted.

How Do I Handle Temptation?

Temptation often tries to draw us away from doing what is right. During high school I had the opportunity to visit the city morgue. We trailed along behind our forensic guide. As we entered the morgue, I was stunned by the sight. People lay on gurneys about the room, tags on their toes and white sheets for clothes. It was quiet. The only response was from one young woman who blurted out, "I think I need to leave!" and dashed out of the room.

I think of those corpses when I read in Romans 6:11 that we are dead to sin. Dead people do not respond. It doesn't matter whether I talk quietly or scream; they do not hear. If I nudge them, they do not move. That's how I should react to sin. Temptation strolls into my life and nudges me; I won't respond. Temptation may even try to argue with me or scream to get my attention. I do not respond—I'm dead to it!

But what about the times when you don't resist temptation? What about the times when you fail? Is there a second chance? Can you influence other women when you carry skeletons in your own closet?

Sometimes, we think, it's too late to make a difference. You may feel you have made too many mistakes with your own life to be an example. If that were true, no one, including me, would ever write a Christian book. But God can overcome any obstacle when we have a yielded, willing heart.

Wilma Rudolph, a world-renowned runner, almost didn't make it to the track. She was born into a poor, black Southern family, the twentieth of twenty-two children. When Wilma was four years old, she was diagnosed with polio, and doctors told her Bible-believing mother that Wilma would probably never walk again. But Mrs. Rudolph didn't think that was God's will for her little girl! So she never gave up hope, and she worked tirelessly to help Wilma not just walk but run.

Wilma clung to her mother's faith. For over six years, she had to wear a cumbersome brace, but one Sunday morning in church, she took off her brace and walked down the aisle unassisted. She went on to become an excellent runner.

At sixteen Wilma captured a spot on the Olympic team. However, she did not live up to her own expectations and captured only a bronze medal in the women's four-hundred-meter relay. Her coach still had high hopes for her future. At sixteen, she still had many great years of running ahead of her.

The next year, Wilma started dating a young man. During a routine physical, she found out that she was pregnant. She herself was shocked. She had been too reserved to ask about sexuality, and her mother had been too reserved to tell her.

This dilemma was hard on Wilma; she had embraced Christianity, and she felt she'd disappointed not only God but her supportive parents as well. Her running coach at Tennessee State set aside a personal rule he had about not allowing mothers to train on his team. "The people I loved were sticking by me, and that alone took a lot of pressure, pain and guilt off my shoulders," said Wilma. She gave up social life in order to mother her baby. She disciplined herself to balance her running, her studies and her parenting.

Wilma secured a spot on the 1960 Olympic track and field team and sprinted into the history books as the first female to capture three gold medals. Her persistence had a snowball effect. Her welcome-home parade was the first racially integrated event in her hometown's history. She opened once closed doors for other women athletes. And she later traveled with the Billy Graham team.

If you fall, don't say, "Oh, well," and use it as an excuse to continue sinning. Just agree with God that it was sin and go on with the new plan. One mistake doesn't mean you'll never get it right. When children learn to walk, they fall down, but they keep on walking. No toddler says, "Well, I fell, so I'm just going to sit here for the rest of my life. It must be God's will." Nope. Success is just getting up one more time after a fall.

What's the Standard?

Excellence connects our priorities to God's. God's Word is the plumb line for our lives. When my husband and I built our home, I helped run the plumb lines. I would hold the top of the string and drop the weight down to see if the wall was square. Bill was meticulous in making sure it was done right. One evening I was getting bored and said so. Bill reminded me that if this step was done wrong, the entire house would be unstable and no amount of paint or decorating could cover up the huge repercussions that would ensue.

It is the same with our own lives. If we use the standards of those around us as the measuring rod for our own excellence, we will be only as good as the company we keep. God has something much better planned for us! Our attitudes, appearance and actions should be based on God's best for our lives. Our professional, ministry and volunteer work should be done well because we are doing it for God. Our parenting and friendships will be strengthened as we treat others as God would treat them. All that we say and do is an offering, a thank-you gift to Jesus for all he has done for us.

Integrity Is a Journey
Sometimes we have the desire to walk with Christ and be our best for him, but old habits nag at us. How can we ditch the old and put on the new self? How can we become comfortable with a holy lifestyle? Here are three steps I have found helpful.

Choose to get well. After my third son was born, I had to come home to an apartment that was in the center of a blasting site. A new development was going in next door and the workers were blowing up the entire mountain to do it. It was mid-August, humid and hot, so we had all the windows open. The noise was horribly loud. My mother and I couldn't even carry on a conversation. To get any peace, I had to shut all the windows. The same thing can happen in our lives.

We are bombarded with lies from the media, society and our own flesh. There is a spiritual battle raging for our hearts and minds. Satan is called a roaring lion, and his goal is to eat us alive. He can accomplish this by getting us to believe lies—lies about ourselves, others or God. The Bible tells us to take these stray thoughts captive (2 Cor 10:5). You can shut the windows. When you fill your mind with the truth, you close off the lies.

So often when we come to Jesus and are trying to break old habits, we focus only on the old. We may say to ourselves, *Don't smoke. See that cigarette—don't smoke it.* Soon we are so consumed with not doing it; "it" is all we are thinking about—and because "it" fills our thoughts, we find ourselves doing the exact thing that we didn't want to!

Instead of focusing on what you aren't going to do, decide what you are going to do in its place. If you don't want to overeat, choose an activity to replace eating at the times you usually fall. If you don't want to drink, don't go to the bar; go to AA or to a friend's home. If you don't want to spend money, don't go to the mall; go for a walk. If you don't want anything to control you, get a plan! Often the external sins are a symptom of an internal problem. You want to have a plan to address the internal hurt as well as the external behavior. If you have an escape plan ready ahead of time, you will be able to cope under pressure. If you fail to have a plan—you're planning to fail.

Change your "pink slip." When you purchase a used car, a pink slip is given to you showing your ownership of the car. When Jesus came into your life, you gave him the pink slip to your heart. He's the new owner. You need to choose to read his owner's manual and run your life according to it. He made you, so he knows what's best for you.

Change is uncomfortable, and it comes with a price. You will have to invest time, money, energy and emotions. The payoffs are great, but only you can make the initial investment. Friends and family may fight the change. Holiness makes the sin in each of us uncomfortable. Sin wants everyone in the mud with it, so when you choose to step out of the mud pit, expect some squealing!

This process is sometimes more effective with help. A trusted friend, counselor or pastor can be God's instrument in helping you succeed in your choice to listen to God's voice. Someone who understands the principles of spiritual warfare can help you learn to respond to God.[2]

Hang on to the lifeline. The cupola of the world-famous St. Paul's Cathedral in London was painted by Sir James Thornhill, and the work had to be done while standing on a temporary platform high above the pavement. One day when he had finished an important detail on which he had spent hours of painstaking effort, he stopped to inspect what he had done. Slowly he began moving backward to get a better view. The man helping him suddenly became aware that one more step would result in a fatal fall.

To startle Thornhill with a shout might also make him topple from the scaffold. Quick as a flash, the helper took a brush and made a sweeping stroke across the exquisite masterpiece.

Greatly disturbed, the artist rushed forward with a cry of anger and dismay. After his companion explained the reason for his drastic action, however, he burst into expressions of gratitude.[3]

Committing to a loving body of believers for fellowship and *continuing* to be teachable and accountable to a few will challenge you to further growth. It can be tempting, after taking the first big step in healthy living and getting grounded in the basics—putting out the fire of our most urgent crisis—to want to run away to a different group of believers who don't know us so well. Sometimes accountability hurts. We feel uncomfortable, so we switch counselors, or we switch small groups or churches, rather than continuing the steep uphill climb to integrity.

So often, when people get close enough to tell us that we are getting ready to step off a cliff, we get angry. Even if we say it in love and commitment, sometimes people don't want to hear they are standing on a cliff! As women of influence, we need to risk being the brunt of anger. Sometimes we will lose a relationship with the person—maybe for a short time, maybe forever. But often, she will listen to us—listen to God's Word and God's love through us—and we will win a friend and her gratefulness. Unfortunately, we just don't know what the final outcome will be.

Sarah approached me one day. She was panicked. She just found out she was pregnant, and she was scared. She had been on a leadership team of ours in the past, and now she was asking for help. She felt she had a weakness where men were concerned, and she felt helpless to choose good guys who really loved and cared for her. Now the consequences of falling for a jerk were putting her life in turmoil. Would I disciple her and help her out of this mess?

I walked Sarah through telling her family of the pregnancy. Shortly afterward, when she miscarried, I went through it with her. In the months that followed, she grew and began making lifestyle decisions that were healthy—till suddenly she began to miss appointments and not finish her assignments. I knew something was awry. Through a bizarre set of circumstances, I discovered she was living with another man and having another sexual relationship—the very thing that she wanted help not to do.

My stomach drew into a knot. I knew I had to confront the situation. I made an appointment and shared my heart with Sarah. She saw what she was doing was wrong, but she didn't want to give it up. I asked her to pray. She said she still wanted to meet with me and do Bible studies, and she was still interested in leadership someday. I had to explain that I would love to do that, and I'd love to help her grow, but I couldn't help her grow if she didn't listen to advice that she knew was true. She'd have to give up sex with her non-Christian boyfriend if I was to continue meeting with her. She said she'd rather have her boyfriend than Jesus and walked out. I cried for her. I had tried to love her and support her. I had made it my goal to be compassionate, not judgmental. She had asked for my influence and now she didn't want it. My prayer became, *God, she can walk away from me, but don't let her walk away from you.*

Learn to Agree with Jesus

"Do you not know that your body is a temple of the Holy Spirit, who is in you, whom you have received from God? You are not your own; you were bought at a price. Therefore honor God with your body"

(1 Cor 6:19-20). Knowing that I belong to Jesus and take him with me everywhere does impact my living.

When I realize that the Holy Spirit is in me, I am often compelled to speak out. I've talked to convenience store owners about their porno racks. I've mentioned to video store owners why I do or do not shop at their establishments. I have been known to take business elsewhere instead of having my car tuned up in a garage with Miss April on the wall. In the same way, if someone acts in a way that is honoring to the Holy Spirit inside me, I affirm them. I write a note to the head office when I'm helped by a particularly helpful employee; I explain to a business owner why I am such a regular customer. I drop the Christian lingo, but somehow I refer to God, or I sign the letter with "God bless" or a verse of Scripture.

Sometimes I don't speak—I just react. My son Zach and I were eating lunch at McDonald's one day when a huge man and his buddies sat down in the booth behind us. They promptly started talking, loudly, and the air was whirling blue with obscenities. Zach leaned over and said, "Mom, can we move? Jesus inside me doesn't like those words." Because Jesus inside me agreed, we moved.

I also need to agree with Jesus when he puts my actions under the microscope. One day, I was at the home of a new friend. We were talking about life and ministry, and our conversation slipped over into commenting on someone's life over which we had no influence. As I walked home from her house, the Holy Spirit convicted me of my sin of gossip. I tried to rationalize it. *God, I'm a leader; I can't apologize for something this petty—she might lose respect for me. God, what if I do apologize and she feels I'm judging her? She might not want to be my friend, and I really want her to be my friend. Really, Lord, it wasn't that big of a deal—we were just sharing our convictions.* But as I walked, I knew I had to call her as soon as I got home, and I had to leave the results to God.

"Jenna, I just had to call and tell you I'm sorry for the things I said about Margaret. It wasn't my place to say them and I am sorry for dragging you into the conversation."

"Pam, I'm so glad you called. I was feeling the same way and I was just standing here deciding whether I should call you." Our friendship was cemented that day because I agreed with Jesus.

Be Honest with Yourself

We want to protect our hearts from the sins that can spread like a cancer and take over the heart. Sometimes we get caught in the act.

A woman stopped at a corner deli to buy a chicken for supper. The butcher reached in the barrel and flung the last chicken he had onto the scales. He told her the weight, and the woman thought for a moment.

"I really need a bit more chicken than that," she said. "Do you have any larger ones?"

The butcher put the chicken in the barrel, then groped around as if he was looking for another. After a few moments, he pulled the same chicken out and placed it on the scales.

"This chicken weighs one pound more," he announced.

The woman pondered her options and said, "Okay. I'll take them both."[4]

God wants to do a great work in our heart. It is these inner attitudes that no one but God and myself can see that are the hardest to get out.

One of the ugliest sins I ever had to confront was my own pride. It seemed that everywhere I turned, God was preaching to me about pride. All the illustrations I heard in sermons, all the topics at a conference I attended, all the conversations with other women of influence centered around pride.

I caught myself wondering how I could be guilty of pride since I battle a self-confidence problem so often. Then God pointed out that an oversensitive low self-esteem is pride inside out. When I battle low self-esteem, I am still focusing on me. I am concentrating on seeking approval and encouragement. My eyes are on my needs. God wants my eyes on him.

During that period of time, God brought to my mind all of the ugly thoughts that I had never voiced but had thought. Thoughts like *Why is she so rich? I think I have the same amount of talent. Why is she teaching? I know as much as she does. Why are you blessing that ministry with huge numbers instead of ours?* Those were awful thoughts to face. By complaining, I had been telling God that his plan was wrong and mine was right. In my heart, I was acting as if God was lucky to have me on his team! I was playing God in my own life because of my pride. That was the same sin that caused Lucifer to fall from God's created plan as the highest and most beautiful angel of God!

My heart was broken over my sin. I got away to a private place with God; I fell to my knees and wept. I listed every good thing, every word and every compliment I could remember and I thanked God for accomplishing it through me—in spite of me. I praised God for dealing with the ugliness of my heart. It was his grace that brought my pride to the surface to be skimmed off. When a goldsmith creates pure gold, he heats up the fire, and the dross and impurities come to the surface. The goldsmith continues skimming off the impurities until he can see his reflection in the gold. That's what I wanted, and God knew it.

God didn't stop there. He stoked up the fire again. I felt that he wanted me to confess this hidden sin. I wanted to just keep going and keep it all between God and myself. I was afraid of the criticism that I might take if I confessed to something so ugly and so petty. After all, I was a leader. I felt I should have had this dealt with long ago. But God laid it on my heart and showed me when he wanted me to confess and to whom—and I did. It was hard.

I was discipling a small group of women, and I shared the details of my confession and restoration with those women. Later, I stood up in front of our congregation on a Sunday night during a sharing time and explained the highlights of what I had learned from God. I knew I was free, because I didn't care if they thought less of me; I knew *God* didn't. My slate was clear. Some criticism did float back to me through the grapevine, but mostly I got personal relief for a burden set down. And there was another benefit: a new transparency developed in others who were following my leadership. Because I was honest in exposing the ugliness of the hidden sin of my heart, others felt free to expose and ask for help with hidden areas they had battled for years.

Live by Grace

My motto is "Conviction and resolve for me—grace for others." Gray areas of holiness are bound to come up in life. Should I dance, or drink, or listen to certain kinds of music? Do I go to the company Christmas party where alcohol is served? Do I wear a two-piece bathing suit? Do I do any work on Sunday? Every day the dilemmas come at us. I have found that the best rule is "If you think in your heart it is sin, it *is* sin." (See Rom 14:22-23.)

My mom used to say, "If in doubt, don't." Go with your own personal resolve, but don't act as if you are now the Holy Spirit in everyone's life. Legalism is living by rules, and grace is living by principles. Your job as a woman of influence is to teach the principles to others and challenge them to apply the principles to their own lives.

Harness Your Freedom

" 'Everything is permissible for me'—but not everything is beneficial" (1 Cor 6:12). Just because I am free to do something, that doesn't mean I am compelled to do it. Sometimes I will choose to rein in my freedom for the sake of another. For example, while I was in junior college, disco dancing was the rage. I loved to dance, and I was good at it. But one night it all changed.

I went to a nonalcoholic teen club. I danced every dance. My plan was, during the break and during slow dances, to share with the men I was dancing with my testimony of what Christ meant to me. After one dance, a young man whispered some very obscene things he wanted to do with me after we finished dancing. I was shocked. I had obviously given the wrong message. I felt confused, guilty, dirty and angry. My heart was pure, but my body had given out an entirely different message!

I felt I had really let Jesus down. I felt like *tease* or *fake* was tattooed on my forehead. The wind had gone out of my sails. I wanted to scream, "Don't you all understand—I really do love Jesus. I didn't mean to be seductive! I want you to know my Jesus—but you can't, I'm standing in your way!" That was my last night at the disco. I left that night with a new mindset. I would give up anything that God and I thought would hinder others from coming to Christ. People's spiritual lives became more important than my rights.

I don't want to be a stumbling block to the gospel. Our holiness protects others. We are asked by God to live by his standards; if we do, we won't be a stumbling block to others who may want to come to him.

As ambassadors for Christ, we are called to balance. Like the apostle Paul, we should want to be "all things to all people, that [we] might by all means save some" (1 Cor 9:22 NRSV). We also want to be careful that the exercise of our freedom does not "become a stumbling block to the weak" (1 Cor 8:9). If we stray too far in one direction, we can become legalistic and set up hurdles for people seeking to reach Jesus; if we stray too far in the other direction, our lives may be no different from those living apart from Christ, and they may never see Jesus in us. We all need balance—and the balance is grace!

Embracing Integrity

A woman walking along a tropical beach noticed a giant sea turtle burying her eggs on the beach. Then, much to the woman's dismay, the turtle turned away from the water and wandered into the jungle. She followed the turtle and found her exhausted and dehydrating. She could tell the turtle was fading fast, and she was concerned for its life.

Gathering some seaweed, she carefully wrapped it around the turtle's shell, carried some water over and poured it onto the turtle's back. Then she ran for the ranger.

The ranger reacted instantly. He raced to the spot in his jeep, grabbed the turtle and flipped it over on its back. He wrapped a chain around the shell, hooked the other end of the chain to the jeep, then gunned the motor and dragged the turtle over the rough terrain to the beach. The turtle's mouth was filling with sand as it bounced across the beach behind the racing jeep. The woman was aghast at the ranger's rough treatment of the turtle. The ranger slammed on his brakes, unhitched the turtle and threw it into the sea.

The stunned turtle floated on top of the water for a few moments, then slowly began to swim, the water reviving her. Then she dove under the water, came back up refreshed, as if she felt safe and whole, and swam out into the sea—at home where she belonged.

Gaining character is sometimes like that. You're not quite sure whether you are being killed or cared for! Learning integrity causes a disequilibrium in your life, and for a while you may feel totally off balance. But to be a woman of influence you have to learn to embrace that feeling of disequilibrium. You have to learn to love change—not change just for the sake of change but change for the sake of growth. Growth is a journey—sometimes over rough terrain and through parching sand. But the journey of integrity will lead you to the refreshing water—to the place where you feel at home.

Living It Out

Are there any areas of your life in which you feel God leading you to repent or make amends? In what areas do you want to raise your standard of excellence? Meet with a trusted friend, mentor or counselor and ask for encouragement for your journey.

Chapter 8

A Woman
of Influence
Is Intense

G AIL DEVERS AND THE OTHER COMPETITORS IN THE HUNDRED-METER dash walked and waited. It had been a photo finish. The instant replay board in the Olympic stadium flashed the images of the four champions. The judges reviewed the tape. The winner was still undiscernible.

The delay was just another opportunity for Gail to marvel at the events of the last year. Walking and waiting were activities Gail didn't take for granted. Just over a year before this race, she had been waiting to hear if she'd ever walk again.

In 1988 Gail set an American record in the hundred-meter hurdles. Then a mysterious illness began ravaging her body. Her hair began coming out in handfuls. Her world went from cloudy to dark as she lost most of her eyesight. Her body shrank as she lost over forty pounds. She lost dangerously large amounts of blood. "My feet were swollen and oozing yellow fluid," she says. "I had little holes all over my feet."[1] Unable to cope, her husband left. Because her feet could no longer bear her weight, her parents moved in with her to care for her. It was humiliating to accept help for even the most basic need—like being carried to the bathroom.

In March 1991 Gail visited a new doctor who recognized the symptoms as a reaction to her radiation treatments for Graves disease. Because she believed God would allow her to run in the Olympics, she had declined the traditional treatment for Graves, a beta blocker, which was on the Olympic banned-drug list. The medical staff was able to revise her treatment, and within a month she walked a lap around the UCLA track, in socks—her first workout in two years.

"I felt I was washed up in track, that there was no way I could ever come back. . . . I was scared. I was just hoping God would save my feet so I would be able to walk again."[2] But Gail prayed. Her father, a pastor, prayed. Her mother and all of her friends prayed. Her coach, Bob Kersee, prayed and believed Gail should come back.

Gail started walking, then jogging, then running. One step at a time, literally, she came back. After each workout, she had to cut off her socks and watch her skin peel off with the cotton. As the coach doctored her feet, he'd keep telling her to keep going, keep believing, keep looking up.

As the Olympics neared, Gail still stayed clear of the medication that would have really helped her Graves. She had pushed through the pain and agony, and she was going to steer clear of any drug controversy. On the day of the big Olympic race, Gail's feet were broken out and she could not feel the pressure of her right foot in the starting block. But when the gun rang out, she instinctively shot into action.

Finally the winner was announced: it was Gail! Officials and camera operators ran to congratulate her for her win. Bob Kersee embraced his courageous competitor, looked her in the eyes and said, "You wanted it. You got it."[3]

Later she told the press, "Use me as an example. When the walls are closing in, when someone doesn't know where to turn, tell people I was there. I kept going. So can others."[4]

So can you—one step at a time.

Success is often possible only with intense action accompanied by persistent will. Persistence is *taking one more step*. Too often, women quit too soon. We want to be a heroine but we don't want to act heroic. The road of intensity is the narrow trail, grown over from disuse, lined with thistles and low-hanging branches just waiting to whip us in the face as we climb toward the top.

The Starting Blocks

Sometimes the starting line is the quitting point! At a Christian conference center, during afternoon recreation time, I proposed an idea to the women who had accompanied me. "See that mountain over there, and see that cross? I know how to get to the top. Does anyone want to go on an adventure? We could climb it—it only takes about an hour or two up and back." Four brave women stepped forward.

After lunch, I confidently marched our little troop across the street and to the trail head—or what I thought was the trail head. We scaled up a brush rabbit trail only to discover a dead end. So we retreated.

"I know the trail is marked with surveyor's ribbon. I really have been here before." I tried to instill confidence into myself as well as this band of women.

"Let's try over here," I recommended. Again we climbed to a dead end.

"How about this way?" asked one.

"Try it!" I said. "And while you do that, I'll climb to the top of this rock and see if I can get a better perspective from up here."

This process went on for over an hour—each of us giving suggestions, taking turns leading, finding dead ends and then trying again. Each of us, conscious of each other's feelings, kept checking on the very real option of bagging the whole idea and going to the store for chocolate. I know I was wondering if my companions might be thinking this was a waste of time—after about the tenth try, I was wondering it myself! But after each try, we'd make a new resolve. None of us wanted to quit.

Finally, we all agreed on one last course of action—and sure enough, at the end of that trail was a very faded piece of red surveyor's ribbon. Now we could climb the mountain.

The climb went very smoothly for the first half-hour; then, as we neared the top, there were no more red ribbons to follow. We decided to split the group into two and both try for a course to reach the pinnacle. I led a few across the face of several huge boulders. As I crawled over one, with my eye on the tip of the cross, I spotted a clear path to our destination. At the same moment, the other leader also spotted the cross and led her group to the top. Sweaty and aching, we stood holding on to the cross as the fresh cool breeze rushed against our faces. We'd made it!

Often it's at the beginning of a new venture that you'll encounter obstacles that seem to scream *Go back!* What makes you want to quit before you get started? Is it the poorly marked trail ahead? Is it the steepness of the mountain? Is it the negative comments from friends or family? Or is it some hidden fear, deep in your own heart? Success starts with the first step. It may take all your intensity just to get into the race!

What Is Intensity?

The moving ballad "Via Dolorosa" plays. The song is the story of Christ's passionate walk to the cross. A beautiful young woman dances to the rhythm. She can't hear the music, but she feels its meaning. Heather Whitestone is deaf. But this night she dances to victory and becomes Miss America.

Her road to victory began when she was a toddler. Her mom was determined to get her little girl off the sidelines and into the mainstream. She used to stand behind Heather and say a word. Heather couldn't run and play until she listened intently and said the right word. Heather went on to learn lip-reading, then sign language. "Attitudes will handicap you more than anything in this world," says Heather.[5]

A poster of Heather wearing her crown hangs in a store in her hometown. The poster says, "They said she would only be able to get a third-grade education. Fortunately, she wasn't listening."[6]

The road was intense, but Heather knew God wanted her to keep going. "We are all worthy to Him."[7] Heather hopes to encourage others to hang in there: "My crown should erase the word 'impossible' from their vocabulary."[8]

Intense women are those who perform diligently, earnestly, strenuously in order to reach a predetermined goal. When one of my boys was a baby, I sat in the rocker, nursing my little one and praying. This calm moment was a welcome relief from the hectic circumstances of my life. Life was coming at me fast, and I had to get ready for it. I turned on a tape. The speaker compared women to boats, saying some women are little rowboats that are easily capsized with only a bucket of adversity, while others are stronger and more stable.[9] As I rocked, I prayed, *God, make me an aircraft carrier, where other women can come, refuel, and be off again to accomplish the flight plan you have for them. Stretch me, fortify me, empower me through your power to be an aircraft carrier.* I was praying for intensity.

As I have conversed with business owners, managers, directors of volunteer organizations and church leaders, the same desire is echoed by all: "We wish we could find people who will stick to the task." Businesswoman Mary Kay Ash says, "A person with commitment is worth one hundred with just an interest."[10] To be a woman of influence, you need more than speculation. You need determination that produces follow-through.

Susan B. Anthony is one woman who understood commitment. Susan was one of several women who were committed to securing women's right to vote. She also stood strong in the temperance movement and fought for abolition.

Susan learned the value of hard work as a child; her chores included baking twenty-one loaves of bread in a day. She learned the synergy of teamwork by working side by side with local farm girls at her father's cotton mill. Often these girls were beaten by drunken husbands, who used their wives' hard-earned wages for more liquor. Susan, seeing the injustice, was moved to take action.

She became a schoolteacher, but her earnings were one-fifth of what her male colleagues received, so she protested. She persisted in visiting Negroes in their homes; she saw the visits as part of her role as a teacher in the community. This brought disfavor, and she was fired. Soon she was made president of the Daughters for Temperance.

In 1852 she was barred from addressing a temperance convention because of her gender. God used this to shift her focus, and she became a driving force behind the women's suffrage movement. Teamed with Elizabeth Stanton, Susan tirelessly worked to gain the vote for women. She traveled, spoke, researched, marched. In 1872 she led a group of women to participate illegally in a national election, to test the right of women to vote under the newly adopted Fourteenth Amendment. She was arrested, tried and fined for the act of civil disobedience. She refused to pay the fine. She declared to the judge, "Resistance to tyranny is obedience to God."[11]

Susan B. Anthony never did cast a legal ballot. Upon her death on March 13, 1906, only four states had granted women the right to vote. However, fourteen years later the Nineteenth Amendment was passed, and all women were guaranteed the right to vote.

Susan was single-minded for over forty years. Many women have difficulty sticking to a task for forty days! The most important priorities aren't measured in minutes, hours or days but in multiplied years.

Stay in the Race

But how do we endure? How do we put up with pressure? How can you bear what your life is requiring you to bear?

Jill Briscoe shares a story of visiting the killing fields of Cambodia. Her translator was a small woman who had lost her mother, her father and six brothers and sisters in the genocide. In this single killing field was a towering monument filled with over nine thousand skulls, including those of the relatives of her interpreter. Jill groped for words to comfort in the face of such tragedy. The Cambodian woman replied, "You in the West, when trouble comes, say, get this off my back, God. We in the East say, strengthen my back to bear it, God."[12]

The apostle Paul understood how to stay in the race: "But we have this treasure in jars of clay to show that this all-surpassing power is from God and not from us. We are hard pressed on every side, but not crushed; perplexed, but not in despair; persecuted, but not abandoned; struck down, but not destroyed. We always carry around in our body the death of Jesus, so that the life of Jesus may also be revealed in our body" (2 Cor 4:7-10). The power to race comes from God himself.

A friend sent me a letter from Colombia shortly after someone living on the same mission compound had been abducted by guerrillas. The letter said, "A few years ago a missionary was taken and later killed. Most feel that this current situation will blow over with time. I hope so. Even so, I feel that it's better to be where I believe God has led me and be at risk than to be safe somewhere else and out of God's will."

At the very core of intensity is the ability to *stay*. It is pitching your tent and dwelling right there in a tough circumstance or responsibility. To be intense means to pull out your hammer and pound in the stakes and move in—and stay till the task is accomplished or the circumstance is seen through. When things get tough we aren't supposed to look for a way out; we are to look for a way to stay under them. If we are in God's will, we have God's promise: "When you are tempted, he will also provide a way out so that you can stand up under it" (1 Cor 10:13).

Keep Your Eyes on the Finish Line

I love to watch the hundred-meter dash. It is such a short race that the competitors stretch and strain to propel every centimeter of their bodies forward. The finish is always dramatic as the runner pushes her chest forward, then throws open her arms as she breaks the tape.

Jesus kept the finish line in sight at Calvary. In Hebrews 12:2 we read, "Let us fix our eyes on Jesus . . . who for the joy set before him endured the cross, scorning its shame, and sat down at the right hand of the throne of God." Likewise, verse 1 urges us, "Let us run with perseverance the race marked out for us." We know that this earthly race has a wonderful and everlasting reward! And, because we were worth it to him and he ran the race for us, we can now race for him.

Listen to the Coach

Each year I help to plan and facilitate our church's family camp. One year, camp came on the heels of months of hectic activity. On the last day of camp, I woke up tired, because God had kept me up most of the night dealing with my attitude. My heavenly Coach wanted to correct a harmful pattern.

I had this overwhelming worry and anxiety for the camp. From all external signs it was going well. People were having a good time, new relationships were developing, significant conversations and decisions had taken place—but I couldn't shake the feeling that I had to make everything work perfectly. If something went differently than I had expected, I felt like a failure.

I struggled, knowing life just doesn't allow for such perfectionism. Then one day, writing in my journal, I realized my problem: As a child, making things right was my role in the family. If my parents fought, I saw it as my job to reconcile them. If my brother or sister felt attacked or insecure, I took on the role of comforter. If Mom seemed shaken, I wanted to be her stability. I thought I had to be in control so chaos wouldn't rule our home. Now I was allowing that old need to feel in control to creep back into my thinking. But God was showing me again what I already knew to be true—*he was in control,* and control was not my job.

God has been working this soul-shattering character trait out of my life. Now when I'm feeling burnout nipping at my heels, I step to the side and listen for the voice of my Coach.

Combating Burnout

Women of influence are women who give a lot to others, but we can't outgive God. When we're feeling burned out—on the verge of exhaustion—God has a plan to restore us. In 1 Kings 18, Elijah accomplished one of the greatest victories of his life. The entire nation was gathered on top of Mount Carmel for a showdown between the god Baal and the true God of Israel. The four hundred fifty prophets of Baal prayed. They prayed all morning. Then they prayed and danced. Then they prayed and cut themselves. They prayed and tried their frantic prophesying! No response. The time for the evening offering rolled around— and still no Baal.

Elijah then took twelve stones, one for each tribe in Israel, and built an altar. He dug a trench around the altar, laid the offering on the altar, then drenched the whole thing with water. Three times he drenched the sacrifice with water. Then Elijah prayed—once—and the fire of the Lord fell and burned up the sacrifice, the altar, the water and the soil! The people fell down and worshiped the true God, and the prophets of Baal ran for their lives. The prophets of God captured them and took them to the Kishon Valley and killed them.

Elijah was exhausted. He climbed back to the top of Mount Carmel, bent down to the ground and put his face between his knees. His day wasn't over! He was praying for rain! Seven times he sent his servant to check for rain clouds while he kept praying. Then it rained.

He urged King Ahab to return to the city in his chariot. Then verse 46 says, "The power of the LORD came upon Elijah and, tucking his cloak into his belt, he ran ahead of Ahab all the way to Jezreel." Jezreel was about twenty-five miles from Mount Carmel!¹³

Restoration Step 1: Pray

At the end of an intense responsibility, there are usually loose ends that need to be taken care of, but no one wants to do it, because everyone is exhausted. We're tempted to stop short. Elijah may have felt that way. A drought was in the land; the people had repented, and so Elijah asked for rain. Not only did he get the rain for the many, he got personally empowered for the next leg of his journey. What Elijah probably felt like doing was taking a nap, right there on top of the mountain! But he made a much wiser move: he prayed.

There are times, because of pressing deadlines, when I have begged God for renewed strength. I might be near the end of a project and feeling sleep-deprived and brain-dead, so I climb in the shower and pray and sing praises. Ten minutes later, I feel like a new woman. However, this is not a lifestyle. I cannot presume upon God's grace to cover for months and years of abuse to my body or slothful management of my time or my spirit. But when I know I have been obedient and given my all, and I'm still coming up short of what it would take to complete a project and glorify God, God does make up the distance.

Restoration Step 2: Prepare for Attack

After you've accomplished something you know was totally through God's power and grace, watch out for flying arrows! Satan wants to rob your joy. He wants to make you ineffective or introspective so that you'll associate negative emotions with doing great things with God. He wants to sideline you in the future by attacking you now.

Elijah's attack came from a crotchety, manipulative woman, Ahab's wife, Queen Jezebel. She put out a death threat! She was mad that her prophets were dead, and she wanted Elijah to pay. Elijah, the man who had just witnessed the huge, miraculous power of God, ran for his life!

He sat under a tree and said, "I have had enough, LORD. . . . Take my life" (1 Kings 19:4).

Elijah's perspective was definitely off! If Satan can't distort your picture of God, he'll distort your view of yourself. We need to never doubt in the darkness what we know to be true in the light.[14]

Restoration Step 3: Put Your Feet Up!

Rest. We all *need* it. Our first weekend in full-time ministry was surrounded by a lot of hoopla. On Friday evening my family flew in, and we decorated the church and hall for my brother's wedding. Arriving at our new little apartment, we saw a throng of people—and most of our belongings flung across the lawn. My new little next-door neighbor, who was about four, came running up to me. "I saw water. It was a big flood! But I got Mr. Manager." I gave her a big hug and kept walking. A few relatives had arrived before us and they, along with the manager, a carpet cleaning team and my mother, were trying to sort through the mess.

We had one hour to be changed and back to the church for the wedding rehearsal. Somehow everyone pitched in, and our wonderful Christian manager whisked us out the door and said he'd handle the rest. We had the wedding rehearsal and dinner until late that evening.

The next day we took care of last-minute wedding preparations, sorted through damp personal belongings, took part in the wedding, came home and cleaned up. On Sunday morning at eight, Bill and I, holding our little six-month-old, Brock, were standing and smiling at the front of the church. Bill was being installed as the new youth pastor, and because the family was all there, we had chosen that Sunday for Brock's baby dedication. We had Sunday school to run, in between the two services, and then we were off to a big family lunch before everyone left town to return home.

At six, we were back at the evening service, then off to a big church staff dinner in honor of our senior pastor's wife. By the time dinner was served, Brock was fussy. Poor guy, he'd been so jostled all weekend that even nursing didn't calm him down. I sat quietly in a room, isolated from the party, trying to feed him so we could rejoin the staff that I didn't even know well yet. For forty minutes I tried twisting God's arm with my theology. *God, you control all things. Make Brock go to sleep!* I finally gave up and took my crying baby to his daddy. Bill encouraged me to get something to eat.

The pastor's wife, Charlotte, met me at the table. Being the compassionate woman that she is, she asked me how I was. I broke down. I recounted the weekend as quickly as I could, feeling guilty the entire time for crying at her birthday party. She lovingly put her arms around me and said something very important: "Oh, honey, you're just tired. A long time ago, a wise woman in ministry told me that tiredness is Satan's tool. She advised me, 'If you are discouraged, take a nap first before you do anything else.' "

Rest includes adequate sleep, nutritious food, exercise and a slower pace of life. An angel of the Lord touched Elijah and said, "Get up and eat." There was fresh bread, straight from the heavenly oven, and water. Elijah ate, then fell asleep again. Later, the angel woke him again and urged him to eat to prepare for the next leg of his recovery.

When we hit times of stress, often we reach for what is easy or quick to eat. These foods too often are not the best nutritionally. Sometimes stress makes us forget to eat all together. Stormie Omartian, in *Greater Health God's Way*, suggests a helpful guideline: eating pure food the way God made it.[15] This simply means avoiding prepared foods and choosing foods that are closest to the way you would eat them if you grew them yourself.

Sometimes the best way to help our body and our spirit to recover is to have a short fast, drinking water only, or maybe just clear juices and liquids, for a day or so. Fasting accompanied with prayer can renew the spirit as well as the body.

In choosing to eat healthy, don't fall prey to legalistic attitudes that would make you think you are more spiritual because you have a certain diet. Good eating habits are important, but so are good attitudes. Elijah took what God gave him and ate it. Elijah didn't go on a crusade to change all of Israel's eating habits. He simply ate and rested in God.

Elijah had gained enough strength to travel forty days and forty nights to the mountain of God. This is the same place where Moses had heard God speak in the burning bush and where the law had been given. Elijah returned to where he knew God had spoken. He needed God to speak to him again.

Restoration Step 4: Pour It Out

God called to Elijah and asked him, "What are you doing here, Elijah?" (1 Kings 19:9). That question wasn't for God's benefit. He knew exactly what Elijah was doing facedown in a cave.

God let Elijah dump. "I have been very zealous for the LORD God Almighty. The Israelites have rejected your covenant, broken down your altars, and put your prophets to death with the sword. I am the only one left, and now they are trying to kill me too" (v. 10).

Well, Elijah had about half the story right. One woman was out to kill him. But he had run away from a revival, not a revolt. God told Elijah, "Go out and stand on the mountain in the presence of the LORD, for the LORD is about to pass by" (v. 11). Elijah was told to get out of the dark, damp cave and stand up in the fresh air of the mountain, and God would meet him there. Often, the most healthy thing we can do when we are depressed is get out of bed!

Elijah stepped out onto the mountain. "Then a great and powerful wind tore the mountains apart and shattered the rocks before the LORD, but the LORD was not in the wind. After the wind there was an earthquake, but the LORD was not in the earthquake. After the earthquake came a fire, but the LORD was not in the fire. And after the fire came a gentle whisper" (vv. 11-12).

When God wants to get our attention, things often get worse before they get better. Sometimes the wind, the earthquake and the fire are within our souls. When we have been burned out, God uses this time to get our attention. Sometimes he shakes the very foundations of our lives so we can see what we've been standing on. Sometimes his fire purges our heart of thoughts, plans and desires that are unhealthy. Sometimes he allows the wind to whip in and carry off anything that is not nailed down in our life. To really restore us, he has to get us pared down to the necessary and the important. Then his gentle whisper will come.

God asked Elijah again, "What are you doing here, Elijah?" (v. 13).

Elijah repeated the exact same answer as before. But God didn't accept it this time. He recommissioned Elijah and gave him a reality check:

Go back the way you came, and go to the Desert of Damascus. When you get there, anoint Hazael king over Aram. Also, anoint Jehu son of Nimshi king over Israel, and anoint Elisha son of Shaphat from Abel Meholah to succeed you as prophet. Jehu will put to death any who escape the sword of Hazael, and Elisha will put to death any who escape the sword of Jehu. Yet I reserve seven thousand in Israel—all whose knees have not bowed down to Baal and all whose mouths have not kissed him. (vv. 15-18)

God restored Elijah's hope by reminding Elijah: (1) You are called and needed. (2) I have a plan for your safety. (3) You are not alone. (4) Here is the network that will support you. Often when we are burned out it's because we aren't believing one of those statements.

Intensity is necessary for influence. Intensity can accomplish what your heart can dream. What is stopping you short? What makes you give up on a plan? Why do you feel exhausted or discouraged? You can be an intense woman. The gentle wind will cool your tired body and calm your frayed nerves. Now turn your face to the Son and take a step—just one step—forward.

Living It Out

Which do you need today: to step up to the starting line, stay in the race, keep your eyes on the finish line, listen to your coach? What step do you need to take to avoid burnout? When I am really under the gun, I copy special verses and sayings that rekindle my strength, and I post them (on bright-colored paper) all over my home. Choose three or four sayings or verses, write them out and post them. Then choose a favorite and mail it to a friend. We all need encouragement for the race!

Chapter 9

A Woman
of Influence
Is Inquiring

ONE DAY, SITTING IN A NURSING HOME, MYRTIE HOWELL PRAYED, *LORD, what more can I do for you? If you're ready for me, I'm ready to come. I want to die. Take me.*

But instead of taking her, God spoke clearly to her heart: *Write to prisoners.*

I said, "Lord, me write to prisoners? I ain't got no education, had to teach myself how to read and write. And I don't know nuthin' 'bout prisons."

She was right. At the time she hadn't heard of Prison Fellowship or any other Christian prison ministry. She wrote a letter and simply addressed it to the nearest prison she knew of: Atlanta Penitentiary, Atlanta, Georgia. Myrtie went on to correspond with hundreds of inmates, sometimes as many as forty at one time. When Chuck Colson went to visit this amazing woman, who was over ninety at the time, she told him, "So, now, Mr. Colson, you just keep remembering the Lord don't need no quitters."[1]

That's the way each woman should move toward heaven: still stretching, still growing, still striving to reach upward and onward to God's glory. Many of us sink into our ruts and cover our heads, waiting for the heavenly trumpet to sound. I once heard that "a rut is just a grave with the two ends kicked out!"

Change is good for women. Change forces us out of our comfort zones so we can fly. When a mother eagle constructs her home, she first lays down briars, jagged stones, all kinds of sharp objects which would seem to be unsuited for her purpose. She then covers this structure with a thick layer of wool, feathers and the fur of animals she has killed. This makes the nesting place soft and comfortable—a delightful sanctuary where she may hatch her young.

But the eaglets will not remain in their inviting cradle for long. The day will come when the mother will stir up the nest. With her sharp talons she will tear away some of the soft, downy lining so that her little ones will feel the sharp edges underneath. The young birds become so miserable that they are willing to get out and begin looking for their own food.[2] Change may feel to you as if your nest is being stolen right out from under you. If so, it's time for you to learn to fly!

Learn Through Experience

My grandfather loves to remind me: "The best way to learn is by doing." Experience is the greatest teacher. A wise proverb says: "Experience is what you get when you don't get what you want. The school of hard knocks is an able teacher." Oscar Wilde says, "Experience is the one thing you can't get for nothing."[3] Others say experience is that "wonderful knowledge that enables you to recognize a mistake when you make it again."[4]

Experience forces theory to work into real life. Experience also gives us insight into what we don't want to do and how we don't want to do it. It was experience that showed me that I love to teach junior high, high school and college, and I'd really rather someone else handled the preschoolers. Experience showed me my heart was with women's issues rather than politics in general. Years of experience on the farm convinced me of my need for a college education majoring in English, not agriculture. I would have starved if running the farm was up to me!

Experience helps us personalize what we do and gives us a methodology for doing it. Because I have had homeless people live with me, I have a philosophy about the homeless. Because I've discipled scores of women, I have a discipleship method.

Because I have worked with women in crisis year after year, I now handle them differently from how I did as a novice. So often I rushed to fulfill the individual's every need and tried to rescue her from her hurt. In my first few years in ministry, if someone called in a panic over her marriage, I felt I had to run right over and solve her problem.

But I learned that if I always pulled a rescue, she never learned to lean on God when she felt panicked. She often didn't finish taking the steps that would lead to the eradication of the source of the problem; she didn't need to, since I would fix things for her. It isn't always wise to rush right in. If a problem has taken years to develop, it will probably take years (and lots of hard work) to get resolved. Rushing in and putting a Band-Aid on a situation doesn't help, especially when God wants to do major surgery. I now realize that I shouldn't work harder at her recovery than *she* is working.

Learn Through a Small Group

Small groups have revolutionized the church. It should be no surprise. Jesus sent his disciples out by twos. The whole group numbered only twelve at first. A small band of women also consistently followed Jesus. He promised, "Where two or three come together in my name, there am I with them" (Mt 18:20).

Small groups can meet to study a specific topic, to meet a specific need, to accomplish a specific task. Small groups can be covenant groups with a goal of mutual accountability and growth. All a small group needs in order to get started is a leader—one person who gathers one to a dozen others together. The reason and focus should be well established. Is this group primarily for Bible study? Is it primarily for encouragement or prayer? Is it primarily task-oriented? Are we gathered to facilitate a skill? How long will it run? Where will we meet? What roles need to be filled, and who will fill them?

Each year, I challenge a group of women to become women of influence. These women share a similar vision for reaching the world, yet many lack training and a facilitator for their dreams. This is my favorite small group. We help each other stretch and grow in some very scary areas, and we become each other's stretcher bearers in the midst of the battle. A member of one of the "Women of Influence" groups told me that she had grown more in one year in that group than she had in her other thirty years as a believer.

I have a network of friends who are committed women of influence. Several of these friendships go all the way back to college, where I was in a small group with a handful of other women who were training for Christian leadership. Small groups provided the forum for those relationships to build.

Grace was the friend who reconnected me to God. In college, we swam on the same team and ministered side by side in Campus Crusade for Christ. She, her husband, my husband and I worked in youth ministry together. Her husband was the official youth pastor when we started, but the four of us grew to be a team. For a while, Bill and I lived in an apartment directly over them. We were all newlyweds with no money but a huge commitment to Christ and a burning vision to see young people transformed for him. We ate together, prayed together, double dated and ministered side by side. Some of my most precious memories of ministry are from those years. What set apart that relationship was the total honesty and transparency that we had with each other. Transparency built week after week as we met together in a small group.

One day, Grace, Steve and Bill and I were planning youth activities for the upcoming year. Steve wanted to take the youth group on a bike trip down the coast of California. I thought it was an outrageously crazy idea, and I spouted off my opinion in a very ungracious manner.

But Steve continued, "It'll be great! The motto can be 'Nothing's Too Tough to Make Me Complain!' "

We all agreed the kids needed to learn that lesson. Then I proceeded to complain about having to go on a bike trip! Finally, the other three were able to get me reservedly on board, but I still had a bad attitude.

The next morning after Bible study, Grace asked me to stay for breakfast. She very lovingly confronted me about my attitude about the trip and the huge lack of respect I had shown. She calmly walked me through the episode and showed me how my words had stung. She was right. I was ashamed, but that conversation was a turning point in our relationship. Grace could lovingly confront—but just as lovingly, she continued to cheer me on, and still does today.

God, having a wonderful sense of humor, wanted to drive home the fact that I was susceptible to bad attitudes. The bike trip was an adventure of a lifetime!

On the back of every shirt was the trip's motto: *Nothing's Too Tough to Make Me Complain!* We had plenty of opportunities to practice using it. The mountains were high and plentiful; the days were too hot and the seats too hard. My thighs burned; my back and arms ached from fatigue.

One young man got lost from the group in a city where he didn't know the destination and had no map. That meant that after a day of biking, some of the leaders had to bike around in a search party! Miraculously, God got him to the right place.

The next day, several bikes (mine included) went over a cliff when the trailer came unhooked. They were retrieved looking more like pretzels than bicycles. Two suitcases washed out to sea in that adventure! There were flat tires, near collisions, cold showers . . . but nothing was too tough to make us complain (much). We worked hard on our attitudes.

That trip pushed me further as a person than any event I've ever participated in. It was the best ministry preparation I've ever received. People want to follow a tenacious leader. I learned how to lead when I didn't think I could go one more minute myself!

An interesting note is that a majority of those who took that trip as young people are serving Christ in ministry today. Grace and I continue to encourage one another up hills much steeper in our lives as women of influence. Years in a small group gave us the beginnings of a strong friendship.

Learn Through Being Mentored

But sometimes we need ongoing help with the process. A discipleship relationship—where a more mature Christian woman *disciples,* or *mentors,* or *trains and encourages,* a younger one—can be the lifeline we need. The goal of discipling is to present every woman complete in Christ so that she can win others to Christ, build others up spiritually and send them out in ministry—so that they in turn can win, build and send.

In the skilled trades, through the centuries, apprentices would train under master craftsmen to learn the intricate methods and secrets of producing exquisite masterpieces. As they worked side by side with the master, day after day, much was caught that was never formally taught. Mentoring can be that way too. Some of my most needed insights have come as a result of picking an older woman's brain. Over lunch, I have the freedom to ask specific and often personal questions that wouldn't be covered in a large-group setting.

There are many kinds of mentoring relationships. Some are short-term and may last only a matter of days or weeks. Others are longer, lasting years. This kind of honest relationship is a safe forum to sift out your thoughts, feelings, hopes, dreams, bad habits and stumbling blocks.

To start on this mentoring process, pray for God's guidance; then look around for possible mentors. Mentors may be busy people who will have to carve out time, or they may be retired and easily able to make time for you. You are looking for an older woman in the Lord. (Older doesn't necessarily mean chronologically. The woman should be ahead of you in her spiritual journey with Christ.)

As you prepare to begin learning from a mentor, ask yourself questions. What exactly do you want to learn from her? How free are you going to allow her to be in commenting on your life? Are you teachable enough to receive constructive criticism as well as praise?

Approach your potential mentor. Ask for a small amount of time, like a lunch or a breakfast first. Sometimes this initial contact will be all you achieve. The mentor may live too far away or have family or work responsibilities that don't allow her to be an ongoing part of your life. Still, much can be learned in a small amount of time. Some of my most treasured conversations have been in the form of letters written to women whom I have respected and who have written back. Several times a mealtime conversation at a conference has profoundly influenced my ministry and career. Sometimes a certain phone conversation was exactly what I needed.

Be specific. Explain why you want to be discipled, why you'd like *her* to disciple you and what you'd like her to teach you. Ask if she would think about it for a few days. Ask for a minimal amount of time at first—perhaps having lunch once a week for four to six weeks or getting together once a month for six months. If the time together proves valuable, then you can both agree to expand your mentoring relationship.

While my husband and I were at seminary, I formed two friendships that have helped me learn the ropes of being a woman of influence.

Phoebe O'Neal was the wife of the dean of Talbot during our first year there. Phoebe challenged a few of us wives to leadership and we spent time, often over waffles, planning out a ministry to reach and equip student wives headed for ministry. But I learned much more from Phoebe. I learned how to keep a heart for a lost world; I learned how to be gracious and hospitable; I learned how to challenge in a way that was nonthreatening yet effective. In the many years since, I have learned from her example and her friendship. She is now a widow, with an entirely different role, yet she's still a woman of influence with a burning passion to reach her world.

My friendship with Sally Conway grew right after her first battle with breast cancer. From Sally I have learned how to keep first things first. Sally has the ability to be perfectly composed when a storm rages around her. People really matter to Sally. She worked hard at helping me form my writing, but I was always more important than my writing. I am a person, not a product, to Sally.

I'd drive all day to spend time with either of these mentors. I come away with a clearer head and a bigger vision after spending time with them. Because they are older and have been through a lot of what is still ahead for me, when they say, "You'll get through this," I actually believe it. When they say they'll pray for me, I know they do.

Learn Through Being a Mentor

Sometimes we know we need help, but we're not sure exactly what help we need. Tricia was like that. When I met her, she was a welfare mom living with a man outside the context of marriage. She was shy and wounded, but I could tell she had a heart of gold and an ability to trust God—when she knew what he was saying to her.

One day, when I was driving her home, she asked if we could meet from time to time; she wanted to know how to pray "right." I was already praying about approaching her to see if she was interested in a discipleship relationship, and her request answered the question. She had lots of questions about God, and we met week after week to answer them. One day, I sensed she was ready to answer one of my questions.

"Tricia, you know God really loves you—right?" She nodded her head. "You know that he wants to give you a plan for your life that will give you a future and a hope—right?" Again she nodded yes. "Tricia, do you think it is God's best plan for you to keep living with a man that you're not married to? Do you think it's God's plan for your kids?"

"You know, Pam, I've been thinking about that. What do you think?" Together we then studied what the Bible said about marriage, commitment, the ability of God to provide. Shortly afterward, I helped her move out and get established in a new life.

Tricia learned God's principles eagerly, and she applied them no matter the sacrifice. I encouraged her as she got into a job training program; I helped her learn how to organize her home and her life; I cheered for her as she led many of her friends and family back to God. I applauded when she eventually married a godly man.

Her oldest children are entering their teen years now, and they have wonderful hearts for God. Their mom has modeled simple and courageous faith in God, and it's passing on to the next generation. She has become a woman others go to when their lives are falling apart. She has also discovered a well of artistic talent that God is using to reach and encourage others. I expect Tricia will continue to accomplish great things for God.

If you'd like to be a discipler but no one has asked you, begin to pray regularly that God will bring you a younger Christian to whom you can give encouragement and teaching. Look around. If you sense a certain woman needs discipling and is open to it, offer such a relationship, on a short-term basis such as one hour a week for six weeks, and make it easy for her to decline if she wishes. God will grow you as you give.

Learn Through Leading

"A disciple is not above the teacher, but everyone who is fully qualified will be like the teacher" (Lk 6:40 NRSV). As you give your life away, women will grow more like you. And you will grow more as a follower of Jesus. Having others following us keeps our hearts and minds attuned to God's and motivates us to be going somewhere! The fact that women will be observing you, asking you questions and imitating your life can be intimidating—but it doesn't have to be paralyzing. Paul said, "Follow my example, as I follow the example of Christ" (1 Cor 11:1).

I like to think of myself as a funnel. Jesus is funneling encouragement, information and guidance through me—but it's Jesus, not me, whom women follow. Most woman don't see themselves as women of influence. That's because they think they have to do some grand thing to be influential. *Being* is much more important than *doing* in a relationship of influence.

Here are four ways to be what a younger Christian needs.

Be prepared. Let her see that you have vision for yourself and for her. Be prepared before your meetings, and expect the same of her. Provide her with extra resources as well as personal insights. Personalize your time with her to meet her needs, as you give her all the basics to help her become a woman of influence.

Be transparent. Share some of your struggles. Allow her to pray for you as you pray for her. Let her know you are only obedient, not perfect. If we aren't careful in this area, we set up the false belief that only a few can really be women of influence. Every woman can influence.

Be available. Open up your life. The more time you can invest, the speedier her growth. Let her see you in all kinds of life circumstances. Let her know when you are available and when you can't be reached. Let her know how to reach you in an emergency, then define *emergency.* You'll only be able to invest in a few women in this way; let these few in closer to your life. Jesus had three disciples, Peter, James and John, with whom he spent extra time. You can't influence everyone, but you can do a good job and influence a few deeply.

Be challenging. Don't be afraid to ask the hard questions. If the woman you're discipling isn't doing her assignments or taking the relationship seriously, talk to her about it. Explain that your time, her time and God's time are too precious to waste. Ask her if she thinks the expectations are realistic. If the relationship isn't working, God may be moving her on to someone who can better influence her—or he may want her to depend more on him and less on a person. These snags are rare, because a person who seeks out your advice and input is usually serious about growth, but if awkwardness does occur, the best course is an honest conversation.

The most difficult decision will always be choosing who to give our lives away to. We can't influence everyone—there is not enough time—or energy! There are two types of leaders; those who like to *build up* and those who like to *build upon*. The "build up" leader can't pass up an opportunity to spend time giving TLC in order to repair or restore. The "build upon" leader focuses on equipping for a task. Both types of leaders love people; they just go about it differently. Some women are better influenced by one style and some by the other.[5] It is good to know your style and make sure those you seek to influence respond well to your style. Choose well whom you mentor.

Jesus spent all night in prayer before he chose the Twelve. Prayer is the key activity when choosing whom to influence. Ask yourself questions: *Is this woman teachable? Is she a natural part of my life? Is she available to meet at times when I am available? Has she shown that she can be faithful? Does she want to influence others?*

Passing the Baton

Passing the baton of influence to the next generation will make you mature. It is an awesome blessing, a "perk" of obedience to God. But it isn't always easy. Sometimes I tire of the hassle of rearranging my life to help others on their journey of growth. When I do, God reminds me that I once was a hassle.

I was an eighteen-year-old with lots of questions, lots of energy and no direction. Tina, the woman who discipled me in junior college, just about gave up on me on several occasions. She was often just trying to get me to date the right men and come to Bible study each week! I was a miserable failure at one of my first ministry jobs—making coffee and cleaning out the coffeepot.

One day, talking with Tina, I ran down the list of excuses why I couldn't keep a ministry commitment I'd made. It was my birthday; my boyfriend was coming from out of town to take me out; he wasn't a Christian so he might feel uncomfortable at the Bible study; I had planned the date before I started discipleship. The list went on and on.

Finally, Tina, grieved in her heart and tired of listening to my pathetic excuses, looked me straight in the eyes and with startling seriousness said, "Pam, who is more important to you, Jesus or your boyfriend?"

"Jesus," I replied.

And the Spirit inside me seemed to whisper to my heart, *Then why did she have to ask?*

For days I was upset. I took a long, hard look at my life. I kept my commitment. The calluses fell off my heart that day. It felt good to put Jesus first.

God often reminds me of that feeling. I recall just why I was willing to pay the price—Jesus paid the price for me first. He went way beyond the hassles, way beyond the hurt, into the very grips of hell to bring heaven to me.

Natural Growth

God created us to grow and stretch. On the farm in Idaho where I grew up, there were two kinds of water. One kind was found in the many ponds that dotted the landscape. The ponds both fascinated and repelled us when we were children. They were filled with fascinating insects and unusual plants. But because their water was stagnant, these same ponds were slimy with moss and sometimes would smell of death and disease. By staying in the same place, this water had become no longer useful, in fact sometimes dangerous. Water was meant to run.

My favorite place to sit on hot summer days was on a wood-plank bridge that crossed a narrow irrigation ditch in our back pasture. The water ran swift and cool. I'd dangle my feet in and dream. I would drop a stick boat in the tiny river and watch it sail downstream. One day, as I dropped in my tiny boat, I thought of where that boat could go. It could float down the ditch and into the canal, and down the canal and into the river, and down the river and into the broad, blue ocean. I wanted to be on that tiny ship!

And, as we follow him and stretch and grow, you and I can sail beyond our horizon and out on God's stretching sea.

Living It Out

Spiritual growth happens in increments. Right now you may need discipleship training that gives you a firm grasp of the basics of the Christian faith, or that deepens your roots in Christ, or that helps you overcome a weakness in your life. You may need training in how to reach out and help others grow. You may need mentoring—time with an older Christian who can help you grow in leadership skills, ministry or career. Or you may be ready to be a mentor and be stretched in the process. What is the next step in your growth?

Check the boxes below that you think will help expand your platform of Christian influence. Then meet a more mature woman for lunch, and ask her what potential she sees in you that could be developed by following one of these steps.

☐ Take classes in _____.

☐ Get a degree in _____.

☐ Teach myself to _____.

☐ Learn about where God fits in my life by _____.

☐ Find someone to disciple me so I can grow. Ask _____.

☐ Find help in overcoming a particular weakness. Ask _____.

☐ Get professional counseling to deal with my troubled past. Call _____.

☐ Find a mentor. Possible women to ask: _____.

☐ Begin to mentor others. Possible women to approach: _____.

☐ Join a small group. Call _____.

☐ Lead or begin a ministry that will equip others. Next step: _____.

Chapter 10

A Woman
of Influence
Is Infectious

THERE ARE TWO WAYS OF SPREADING LIGHT: TO BE THE CANDLE OR THE mirror that reflects it."[1] The best gift God can receive is you—wholeheartedly, unreservedly you! There is no stopping a heart that is wholly his. If we are fired up for God, we will influence others naturally. Being fired up isn't just a state of mind! No, being aflame for God is the overflow of a life plugged into God. When my heart matches God's heart, I will make a difference, because I will be reflecting God's image.

Infectious Attitude

God doesn't need your ability as much as your availability. He can easily equip you. You don't just *have* a ministry—you *are* a ministry! If you decide to, you can be a "contagious" follower of God who influences others constantly as you go through the life to which God has called you. Jesus ministered as he traveled—even in everyday situations. He touched lives as he went from task to task, place to place.

Karly asked me to disciple her at a really busy time in my life. I really did want to spend time with her, because she reminded me of myself before someone made a space to disciple me. Since my schedule was already booked solid, I was honest with her: "The only way I can spend time with you is for you to just come along with me where I need to go." She agreed. So, we have traveled together. Karly has cared for my children. We've folded my laundry, had meals together—and she has become like a daughter to me. I would have missed one of the biggest blessings in my life had I said, "No, I'm too busy." I am convinced that the future will continue to show that it was time well spent as Karly continues to grow and blossom.

Tenacious Flexibility

Your infectiousness will spread when you are flexible and tenacious in seeking to be an influence. Infectious women have a "can do" attitude. Many women let an apparent obstacle stop them dead in their tracks. Don't give up personal growth and ministry too easily. If you can get out of the house to meet a friend for lunch, you can be available for ministry! If you have a half-hour for a phone chat with a friend, you can do ministry. If you have time for a hobby, you can do ministry. Yes, you may have to be more creative in the ministry obligations you commit to, but you can be a woman of influence.

One woman, married to an unbelieving husband, approached her pastor and asked that she be allowed to meet with any woman who came to him for counsel concerning an unbelieving spouse. She loved her husband, but he allowed her only one hour of worship a week. She was, however, free for ministry Monday through Friday during her lunch hour. She developed a lunch-hour mentoring ministry with other women like herself, encouraging them in their personal walks with God.

One day I exclaimed to her, "That must be so hard!"

She replied, "Sometimes it is. But I can't outgive God. He enriches me as I give to him. I won't use my circumstances for an excuse—God is bigger than that." Is there someone in circumstances similar to yours who needs to be encouraged?

Cynthia McKinney is a successful M.D., practicing in Escondido, California. She is young, beautiful, talented and confident. In meeting her, one might think the obstacles she had to overcome to gain her goals were race, gender or economic issues. But (as for most women) it was Cynthia's own self-confidence that was the hurdle.

"I had to learn to believe God at his word and believe verses like Philippians 4:13 are true. It was realizing that God always honors his Word. I had to take the Bible and make it personal. It is knowing the Lord is behind me and knowing that if I'm delighting myself in him, then he'll give me the desires of my heart."[2]

Cynthia is a vivacious African-American Christian woman in the male-dominated world of medical science—and her patients love her. She loves with Christ's hands, and she speaks up for him when he leads. Do you know someone who needs to be reminded that God values her?

You might think you don't have much to offer. Charla Pereau felt that way once. In 1966 she was a homemaker on vacation with her husband, Chuck. They toured the sights of Mexico. Being architecture buffs, they looked up a old abandoned gambling resort in Baja. But as they looked around the beautiful building, they couldn't help but notice all the children in need. Eleven months later the Pereaus purchased that land, and today they run "Foundation for His Ministry," a "by faith" organization seeking to meet the needs of children. Each week about a thousand children are ministered to through Child Evangelism classes sponsored by the orphanage. Thousands of women and children receive care at the clinic. Charla's "ordinary" skill at child care turned into a very significant ministry.[3] Do you have a home to share?

You might be feeling overwhelmed by your own life. Being the mother of preschoolers is a challenge, especially if you have several in diapers at once. One day, a group of eight moms in a local church, frantic to cope, got together in the home of one of the women. As they talked, they realized that their need was common to women, and for the next few years they stuck together and worked out a format that has exploded into MOPS (Mothers of Preschoolers), with over 860 groups meeting in ten countries. Do you have a friend who needs a call from you?

Shirley Johnson is a woman who won't let her disease beat her. Diagnosed with multiple sclerosis, Shirley went from an athletic and active life—she was a piano teacher and Bible teacher—to lying in bed with the use of only her right hand and her mouth. For a time she continued teaching Bible studies in homes with the use of a specially designed car. When her body no longer allowed that, she became a phone counselor for the *700 Club,* and when her voice grew weak she took to writing hundreds of notes of encouragement a month. Maybe you can't do everything you used to do; what *can* you do?

Something to Celebrate

Celebrations are contagious. Parties attract people. If you love life, people will want to be around you, hoping that your enthusiasm will rub off on them. In January 1995, Super Bowl fever hit the streets of San Diego. The stadium was packed to welcome home the Chargers after their AFC win. Lightning bolts were everywhere: worn on lapels, displayed in hotels, painted on cars, fire trucks and puppies! In fact, 55,000 people showed up to wear blue-and-gold T-shirts and make a "human bolt" that was photographed from the air. Many even came the night before and slept in a chilly parking lot to participate. There were singing and dancing and cheering everywhere for two weeks—over a football game.

People like to be part of a winning team. As believers, we *are* a winning team. If anyone has something to sing about, if anyone has reason to tap their toes or cheer—*we* do.

We should look for reasons to celebrate—a raise, a promotion, an A on a paper—even a good hair day. Our family has adopted the tradition of throwing an "Angel Party" when someone comes to Christ. This is taken from Luke 15:10 where the angels rejoice over one person's conversion—they have a party! My kids love for Mom and Dad to influence others, because they get to party. And the enthusiasm is catching—the boys want to share Christ too. You can find your own way to celebrate your influence and get those close to you involved in the issues of your heart.

I started noticing how enthusiasm for life started infecting others when I was in junior college. One morning at six, I carried my breakfast tray through the cafeteria line as I'd done all year and, as usual, greeted the workers. One of them said, "You are always smiling—what makes you so happy at this time of the morning?"

This was one of the first "silver platter" opportunities to share my faith.

I said, "You really want to know?"

"Sure," was the reply.

"I know Jesus personally, so I am confident that today will be a good day—no matter what happens."

That scene has repeated itself over and over again.

Several families have come to Christ as a result of our friendships with them. Many of them are amazed that we act like normal human beings: we tell jokes, laugh, go to ball games, enjoy movies and barbecues and life. After we wrote *Pure Pleasure,* the comment we heard most often was "Wow, I didn't think married Christians *had* much sex, let alone *enjoyed* it!" When our non-Christian friends are honest with us, they'll say, "You guys are real—and you're fun." Somehow Christianity has taken a bad rap, but Jesus brought joy—so can we!

Infectious Home

My children have benefited from our open-home policy. They have watched godly dating relationships develop. They have heard men and women speak of God's calling on their lives over Sunday dinner. Their baby sitters have been wonderful Christians, some of whom have gone on to do exciting things for God.

They have also seen the ugly consequences of sin. They have come to hate alcoholism, drug abuse, abortion and domestic violence, because they have seen the victims left in the wake of these sins. I cannot fully shelter my boys from the pain of sin, nor do I want to. I want them to see that choosing sin is choosing a downward spiral. However, I'm careful to maintain their personal privacy. Kids are still kids. Even when you are committed to being a woman of influence, they shouldn't pay the price for your commitment.

Recently, my son Brock was awarded a new bicycle as a community leadership award because, on several occasions, he had voluntarily given up his own bedroom to help homeless young people trying to get a new start.

What the newspeople didn't know is that he has given up his room all his life—for students in transition, missionaries on furlough and battered women. Each time, we explain to Brock that it is optional for him to lend out his room for a day or so (once for several months). But each time, Brock has responded with, "Sure—seems the least I can do."

Having an open-home policy can bring the best of ministry to your doorstep. Your children will be infected with a desire to help change their world. Discipleship can seem hereditary. Those children who had parents who mentor and disciple are more likely to seek out mentors. They are also more likely to become mentors, because they have seen that pattern modeled.

Infectious Purpose

And the whole process is a chain reaction.

Brenda, one of the first high-school students I ever discipled, has shared Christ with far more women than I, and she will continue to do so. Brenda is now an at-home mother who volunteers for work in women's ministry, and because it is a conviction and a lifestyle, she is always discipling someone.

Brenda grew up in a solid Christian home. When she was a junior in high school, I challenged a small group of girls, including Brenda, to form a discipleship group. For over three years, I spent time with these young women, pouring into their lives all I knew of God and training them to pass on the basics to others and influence their world. "It was this training, the *whys* of Christianity, that stuck with me and became a basis for my life," says Brenda fifteen years later.

Brenda discipled Alison, a high-school senior. Alison has gone on to disciple others and is currently serving with her husband on the staff of Athletes in Action, an arm of Campus Crusade for Christ. Alison says:

There was a turning point in my life. One afternoon, Brenda laid out for me the principle of reproduction. She said, "I'm discipling you, and someday you'll be discipling and teaching others." My first reaction was, "No way! I could never teach anyone!"—but that's what I'm doing.

Alison explains that accountability was the difference. "I had head knowledge, but Brenda was the first person who made it real and practical in everyday life. And she was a good friend."

Backing up a bit: Faith Myatt, a homemaker and lay worker, discipled Tina Wilcox, who then went on staff with Campus Crusade for Christ. Tina is the woman who influenced me so much. The baton of faith was passed from Faith Myatt to Tina Wilcox, to Pam Farrel, to Brenda Cory, to Alison Buchanon, and it keeps getting passed on from person to person, generation to generation. If you can be a friend, you can influence. *Influence is a relationship with a purpose.*

Infectious Lifestyle

We are not meant to reach out only to younger believers. We can make contact with non-Christian women, as well, and be part of God's means of bringing them to faith.

Many Christians run from the world, fearing contamination. But the "contaminant" the world needs is the truth of the gospel—and we are the ones to spread it. We have a contagious hope, a contagious strength, a contagious joy. We need to run into the world. The world desperately needs to rub shoulders with us. Our lives need to be open to others as we work in retail, business, entertainment, education, science, medicine or ministry.

And it's not as hard as you may think. To be effective in reaching and influencing a woman who doesn't know Christ, you need only to do three simple things:

1. Meet her.
2. Answer her questions.
3. Be available to her.

Meet Her

Some of us don't influence the world around us because we aren't out in it. We may go only to Christian functions. We may work for Christian companies and organizations. We may have only Christian friends. We have to get out of our safe Christian environment and simply meet people.

Meeting people in a neutral environment is best. We may have come to Christ from a gang or drug culture, so we are afraid to go back lest we fall into those same temptations. That is a valid precaution, but it doesn't have to stop you from ministering. There are outreach groups that minister to people through gyms, through food and clothing distribution or educational opportunities.

We can meet new people at the park, at the laundromat, in our volunteer work, through children's activities or hobby groups. We need only navigate out a little from our comfort zone. My favorite place to meet people is through education. I love classes, debate and tutoring.

I like to know I have some kind of ongoing relationship with the people I want to reach. I also like to meet other parents through my children's school activities and sports teams.

I look for strategic ways to alter my schedule to allow more people into my life. I enjoy aerobics, but instead of going to a church-sponsored class, where most of the women would be believers, I go to a secular gym. I already love to entertain, so, instead of inviting just Christian people, I'll carefully mix a party or invite all unbelievers. As my life changes with new obligations and responsibilities, I am careful to maintain a balance of influencing the world and influencing believers.

Jo-Anne Cinanni personally led more than forty friends to Christ in a six-year period. Jo-Anne met most of her friends through her second job at a diet and nutrition center, where she works eight hours a week. Her motto: "Preach Jesus. But if at all possible, don't use words." Jo-Anne is convinced that words are a natural outflow of a heart connected to Christ's. She says, "Jesus illustrates how we are to step into the world, reach out to sinners, and relate to them through our hearts in order to minister to them and show them God's love."[4]

Answer Questions

Helping friends with questions is much easier than it appears. I don't have to know all the answers; I only have to be available so my friends feel they can ask me questions. I can always say, "Great question. Let me do some research and get back to you." The bigger obstacle is allowing time for the relationship to develop to the point of trust. It is easy to maintain a superficial air with new relationships. Time, a good listening ear and a few well-chosen questions to get a friend talking are vital. I don't want to seem like a quiz show host to my friends, but I do want to find out what they know about Jesus, what their personal needs and desires are, what their basic personality is. Does my new friend need intellectual answers to her skepticism, emotional answers for her heart or practical answers for her daily life?

In college, as a reentry student, I took a class in women's studies. The professor was a wonderful woman who encouraged free expression and debate. One day she walked in and started the class with a provocative question: "Today we are going to talk about when we first became sexually aware. Who wants to share first?" The class sat in nervous silence.

"Okay, I'll share," I said. I went on to explain how I came to Christ and that because of my trust in his love to me, I followed the guidelines in his book. I carefully chose my words so that I was sharing my experience and not judging anyone else. I shared that I had struggled with maintaining my virginity but in retrospect was glad I had done so. I explained that one benefit of that decision was the strong verbal communication that I now had with Bill. Our communication strengthens our intimacy. We can talk about anything, including sex, and as a result, we have a very enjoyable sex life.

I was interrupted by an angry voice just behind me.

"You narrow-minded bigot! My mother tried to cram that religious crap down my throat, and now you're trying to do it too!"

Inside my heart, I panicked for a second. Then, because I feel securely loved by God and securely called to share him, I responded without defense and with grace. I turned toward her and apologized. I explained that I didn't mean to sound harsh. It was just my experience, and it had worked for me. I smiled and my heart reached toward her. I felt compassion for my attacker, because she obviously was hurting and carrying around a lot of pain.

Hands shot up around the room. Other students, who I didn't even know were Christians, began to share their experiences. One young woman shared that she had been sexually active with men but recently had come to Christ and was happier now, remaining pure and trusting God's plan for future sexual relationships.

During the break I got to talk to many people about God and his love. After class I had a great heart-to-heart chat with my professor. My professor wondered if I was okay. I got to explain that I didn't feel my classmate was lashing out at me but at what I stood for. I shared my heart for women and men who have been hurt by legalistic religion, and I shared my spiritual journey. And my professor shared her own spiritual background and some of the questions she still had about God and Christianity.

In the classes that followed, I even got a few opportunities to talk with my classmate who had been so upset at me. I don't have all the answers, but I know what Jesus has done for me. God just wants us to share our story.

Be Available

On the last day of class in Victorian Literature, we were discussing Joseph Conrad's *Heart of Darkness*. Early in the class, I shared some relevant information on one of the passages from a Christian perspective. The last comment of the day hurt me to the core.

A young woman in the back of the classroom raised her hand and said, "It seems like those who claim to have a 'heart of light' really have hearts of darkness, and those who are told they have dark hearts, like the natives, have enlightened hearts. It's just like Christian missionaries: they go into tribal cultures and push their 'gospel of light' and it exploits the people."

Now some of my dearest friends work with tribal people on the mission field, and I know they aren't there exploiting the people. I know some horrible things have been done in the name of Christ, but for the most part, missionaries through the ages have brought health care, economic enrichment and hope.

True, some of the tribal customs are changed when the tribes come to belief in Christ. In the tribe where my close friends work, the tribespeople used to have the custom of hanging girl babies out in the forest for animals to kill. This practice developed because of a unique custom. The parents of the bride had to arrange a marriage and pay an often expensive and elaborate dowry. This obligation was overwhelming for many parents, so instead of having to face it when their newborn girl grew up, they would carry her into the jungle in the cover of darkness and leave her hanging in a tree for the wild animals to devour.

There is now a severe shortage of grown women in that tribe. Many men long for a wife and family, yet there are not enough women. But because many in the tribe have come to Christ, young girls' giggles again echo in the rain forest, instead of their desperate cries for help.

As I sat there in class, all these things and more were buzzing in my head. My heart was pounding as I tried to gather my thoughts and raise my hand.

Just then the professor said: "Good point. With that comment we will conclude our class. Thank you for attending. It has been nice having such a bright class. Have a nice summer."

Good point? Have a nice summer? That was not a good point! I can't have a nice summer when this class ended in such darkness! Oh God, I let you down!

I gathered my composure through prayer and thanked the professor for all his hard work, but before I got out of the classroom tears were running down my face. *I'm so sorry, God! All semester I tried to represent you. Nearly every class, you gave me the opportunity to correct theology or make a point of logic. Now to have it end this way—it's too hard!*

I got in the car to drive to a creative writing class that I was to teach. I was crying so hard that I could barely see the road. I felt brokenhearted over my inability to find the words I needed.

Then God reminded me of a promise from Matthew 10:19: "Do not worry about what to say or how to say it. At that time you will be given what to say." God will give me the words. All semester God had given me the words. All semester God had given me the opportunity. Today, God had given me neither. I was available, but God did not choose to use me. Using me was God's responsibility. Being available was my responsibility. A sense of freedom flooded me. I held tight to that feeling. I also held tight to the utter brokenheartedness that I was experiencing.

God, please don't ever let me forget either of these feelings. To influence the world, I have to cry over it. But to influence the world, I also have to let you be free to be you—and I have to let myself be free to be me. I won't take your part. I'll just be available to do my part.

Now's the Time

When Jesus left this world, he gave a Great Commission: "All authority in heaven and on earth has been given to me. Therefore go and make disciples of all nations, baptizing them in the name of the Father and of the Son and of the Holy Spirit, and teaching them to obey everything I have commanded you. And surely I am with you always, to the very end of the age" (Mt 28:18-20). This command is for every person who knows Jesus Christ personally. He didn't say only pastors should make disciples, or only directors of women's ministries, or only executives. You might be asking, "Where are the ordinary women? This book is full of extraordinary examples—what about me?" That's just it: we are *all* ordinary, but God is extraordinary!

Every Christian woman is to be a woman of influence. Every woman is to make disciples. Every woman is to go into the world and make a difference for Jesus. Whatever your gifts are, use them. Whatever your platform or office or experience, use it. The two key verbs are *go* and *make disciples.*

Don't wait for women to ask you to mentor them; challenge women to be mentored. Don't wait for a woman to challenge you to be mentored; ask her to mentor you. Don't wait until women in the world ask you for help; offer it ahead of time. Don't wait until they ask about Jesus; go tell them.

No Excuses!

When I was in high school, to get a hall pass to go anywhere you had to ask for an "excuse." Some students made it their ambition to secure as many excuses as possible, in order to get out of responsibility. Responsibility is hard. Responsibility will change your life.

We might not want the hassles of influence. If you have tried to be a woman of influence, you know it is a struggle. People have problems. Problems are a hassle. Sometimes it is a hassle to care.

Kay Cole James went on television for a late-night debate representing a local prolife action. Cards and letters poured into the National Right to Life office lauding her abilities. The leaders of National Right to Life came to her house one evening for dinner, watched the tape and offered her a job on the spot. Kay turned them down. She was a successful businesswoman and mother, and she didn't want to further complicate her life.

A few months later, she was listening to a tape in her car. An Episcopal priest gave a compelling call to involvement in the prolife movement. Kay describes her reaction: "It occurred to me that while this battle for the lives of millions of unborn children was going on around me, I could not hide myself behind a good job selling stereos and TV sets. Babies were dying because people like me didn't want to get involved."[5]

Kay became the national spokesperson for the National Right to Life committee. She was so successful that soon Planned Parenthood representatives refused to debate her. She was a committed, articulate black woman with a passion.

Soon that passion was noticed by the Republican party. One day she stopped by the Bush election campaign headquarters in Washington, D.C., to talk over some issues close to her heart. When George Bush Jr. heard she was there, he approached Kay and asked her to come on board with the new administration.

Kay stalled. She explained that her mother was ill with cancer and it just wasn't a good time. Then Kay went on to visit her mother in the hospital. Kay shared the exciting offer and told her mother that she'd turned it down.

Her mother replied, "Girl, what's wrong with you! I raised you better than that! The son of the president of the United States asks you to serve your nation and you say no! How many people do you think get that opportunity? How many black folks you think being asked?! Girl, you bes' get back on that phone and tell him you was just kidding!"[6]

A mother's affirmation was all Kay needed to plunge her into a life of political service. She joined Louis Sullivan, who was cabinet secretary for Health and Human Services. Later she became a lobbyist in Washington for the Family Research Council, then went on to be secretary of health and human services for Governor George Allen of Virginia. A woman without excuses is free to soar.

Message in Marble

I love traveling the Northeast. History comes alive in places like Boston, Lexington and Concord. One fall, while visiting the area, I walked in a graveyard next to a church. The day was crisp and blustery. The air had an edge to it. I wandered through the cemetery, pushing the multicolored leaves from their resting places on the headstones. These marble headstones were magnificent works of art. Words were chiseled into the stone. It was as if the person's life was the chisel in the artist's hands. The inscriptions chiseled their way into my heart. The personal qualities and major life achievements of the dead were etched there for all future generations to see. *This is what was important to her, this is what she lived for, this is who she lived for.*

What a privilege to be the artist, chisel in hand, tapping out tributes. The careful tapping of hammer against chisel created a permanent monument. These were not cold stone markers symbolizing death, but tributes memorializing life. I wondered, *God, at the end of my life, what will be etched in my stone?*

God moved within my heart: *Pam, you are writing your stone today. Write wisely.*

I leaned back on a tree and, gazing at the nearest tombstone, tried to think of what God would chisel on the marble about my life:

Here lies Pamela Farrel . . . tap . . . tap . . . She believed God could do exceedingly abundantly beyond anything she could ask or think . . . tap . . . tap . . . She loved her husband, her children, her friends and relatives . . . She encouraged women to be all God created them to be. It is with each day of life that we chisel our influence into the hearts and lives of others. Christ is the artist. You are his tool. Only you can decide how you will allow the Master Craftsman to use your life. "One can not transform a world except as individuals in the world are transformed, and individuals cannot be changed except as they are molded in the hands of the Master."[7]

You and I must decide whom we are called to influence. Are our gifts and talents being used only for momentary popular recognition— or is our influence carving out influence for Christ for generations to come? Who are we living for: ourselves or the Master Craftsman, who made us? You are a woman of influence . . . the Craftsman is working . . . tap . . . tap . . . to make a difference.

Living It Out

What do you want on your headstone? On page 173, write three to five sentences that capture what's on your heart.

Now make a list of people who need the influence of God given through you. Choose one person or one group, and create a plan for being a woman of influence.

Discussion Questions

Below are questions for use in small group discussions. You can easily adapt them for one-on-one discipleship or mentoring relationships. Also included is a "Still More Influence" section for those who are currently leaders of women. Your continued growth and encouragement is vital! Suggestion: Jot your answers in a notebook as you go along.

Chapter 1: A Woman of Influence Is Impassioned

1. Respond to this statement: "I'll know what to live for if I know what I'd be willing to die for."

2. The author makes the case that certain elements of passion are unique to each person. Have each member of the group complete this statement for every other member of the group: When I think of _____, I think of _____ and I appreciate that attribute because _____.

3. Have group members share the results of their "Living It Out" exercise. Get feedback from the other members of the group on what "calling" or passion each is carrying.

☐ How does your special passion affect your life today?

☐ How do you feel about carrying the burden for the passion that God has given you?

☐ What changes would you like to make in order to carry out your passion?

Still More Influence: Often the people that God brings into our lives early on have a dramatic role in helping us hear the call of God on our lives. Have you called or written those who influenced you and thanked them for the role they played in preparing your heart for God's impassioning?

Chapter 2: A Woman of Influence Is an Individual

1. Pass a hat to the first group member you'd like to have share and ask: "Which hat, or leadership style, do you think fits you best? Why?" Have each member share in turn.

2. Where do you think your style of leadership would be most effective?

Take this survey:

a. The age groups I like to work with best are: (list three)

b. I prefer to: (choose one)

☐ work alone

☐ work independently but be part of a team

☐ work as a team

☐ work as the boss of the team

c. I love work or ministry best at this stage:

☐ the dream, when everything is still in its planning stage

☐ the ground floor, when the foundation is being laid

☐ the well-oiled machine, when most of the kinks are gone and there is a smooth, predictable system

☐ regrouping, when problem-solving or new ideas are needed

d. I prefer to be accountable for growth to:

☐ one other person

☐ small group of 2-3

☐ small group of 4-7

☐ small group of 8-10

☐ large group of more than 10

e. I like being in charge of or responsible for:

☐ no one

☐ one other
☐ small group of less than 5
☐ medium group of 6-20
☐ large group of over 20
☐ large group of over 50
☐ the larger the better

3. Do you see yourself as a leader? Why or why not?

Still More Influence: Are you being the leader God made you to be? Are you feeling constrained by unrealistic expectations, either your own or others'? List all your leadership roles of the past. Which were the most fruitful? Which were the most fulfilling? Ask God if this is a time to shift how you lead or whom you lead.

Chapter 3: A Woman of Influence Is Intimate with God

1. How do you nourish your intimacy with God daily?

2. Which Bible study method mentioned in this chapter was new to you? Which of the quiet time ideas did you like best? Have the group bring all of their Bible study tools to group one day. Have them practice using commentaries, encyclopedias, word helps and so on. Or take a field trip to a local Christian bookstore, and try out some research tools and computer Bible-study tools.

3. The author quoted J. Oswald Chambers: "Your worth to God in public is what you are in private." Do you agree with that statement? Can you contrast a time when you were running on empty with a time when you ministered out of a full reserve? What new investment do you think God wants you to make in your relationship with him?

Still More Influence: Plan a group quiet time or special worship service for you and the one(s) you are influencing. Let others in on your personal time with Christ. Consider giving a copy of your favorite devotional or Bible-study tool to the one(s) you influence. With the gift, include a note explaining the value of the tool to you.

Chapter 4: A Woman of Influence Is Idealistic

1. Can you be an idealist and a realist at the same time?

2. What character trait of God do you need a better view of? Why?

3. Here are some verses that explain how God sees you. Look them up and note anything you see that answers these two questions: What does God's Word say about you that is especially *encouraging?* What does it say about you that is *hard to believe?*

Exodus 22:31	1 Corinthians 3:17; 4:10
Deuteronomy 7:6; 14:2	Galatians 3:26; 4:7
Matthew 5:13-14	Ephesians 1:1; 2:6; 3:12; 5:8
Luke 12:24	Colossians 2:10
John 13:35; 15:3, 5, 15	1 Peter 2:9-10
Romans 8:1-2	

Still More Influence: Are you modeling a big view of God to those in your sphere of influence? What can you do to gain a bigger view of God? Look up these verses for inspiration:

1 Samuel 14:6	Luke 1:37; 18:27
1 Chronicles 29:11-12	John 1:3; 9:33; 15:5
Job 26:7; 41:33; 42:2	Romans 11:33
Psalm 139	Ephesians 3:20
Isaiah 40:12-31	Colossians 1:16-17
Matthew 19:26	1 Timothy 6:16
Mark 9:23; 10:27; 14:36	

You may want to create your own love letter from God, using verses that have been encouraging to you.

Chapter 5: A Woman of Influence Is Interdependent

1. Which "one another" in the chapter is most difficult for you? Which is easiest? Why?

2. Everyone has a few people in their life whom they just can't seem to understand. What did you learn from this chapter that can help you deal with those people who are tough to love?

3. Relationships change. How do you decide whom to let out of your life and how to do it? Read how Paul handled his departure in Acts 20. How can you apply his example to your own life? (Idea: Make the closing meeting of your group special by celebrating with an overnight trip, a tea or a special event that you attend together. Allow time for each member of the group to affirm the others.)

Still More Influence: Some women you will seek to influence may need the wisdom of a professional Christian counselor. Do you have a list of resources and people that you can refer others to? Start a list by talking to those in leadership positions in churches and parachurch organizations. Network with those in Christian publications and bookstores. You may want to become acquainted with counselors in your area to see which ones you can recommend with confidence.

Chapter 6: A Woman of Influence Takes Initiative

1. Respond to this question: Is it possible to both be spontaneous and set goals?

2. Name one woman, someone you know or have heard of, who has set a goal and made it. What were the steps she took to get there?

3. What is one goal you'd like to accomplish this next month, semester or year, and what step can you take today to help make it a reality? This is a good time to share goal worksheets with a mentor or other group member. You may choose to exchange goal sheets and use them as a prayer reminder for the others.

4. How can you have goals for yourself if other people's needs seem to control your life? How can you have goals that affect others but still do not cross over the line of trying to run their lives? How do you maintain that balance?

Still More Influence: Sometimes trying to discern whether a plan is God's idea or our own is difficult. If you are really struggling with a decision, study these verses for help:

Genesis 11:16; Jeremiah 29:11 Does the plan I have in mind bring unity and hope?

Proverbs 12:15 Am I righteous and are my plans from a righteous heart?

Proverbs 15:22; 20:18 What does my godly counsel say? Have I asked several godly people their opinion?

Proverbs 16:3; Isaiah 5:19; James 1 Is the plan committed to God?

Isaiah 32:8 Is the plan noble?

Jeremiah 29:11 Will the plan bring welfare and hope?

James 1 Will the plan deepen my character?

Matthew 11:29 Is the plan a bearable load?

Romans 12; 1 Corinthians 12 Does the plan make best use of my gifts?

1 Thessalonians 4:1 Will the plan help me to excel still more?

Romans 14:23 Does the plan require faith?

1 Chronicles 28; Job 17:11; 23:14; 42:2; Psalm 20:4-5; 37:4; Proverbs 14:22; 16:1, 3, 9; 19:21; Amos 3:7; Micah 4:17; Romans 15:24; 1 Corinthians 14:33; Ephesians 1:11; Colossians 3:1-2, 15; 2 Timothy 3:16 Are my basic desires the same as God's?

Chapter 7: A Woman of Influence Has Integrity

1. First Corinthians 10:23 says, " 'Everything is permissible'—but not everything is beneficial." How do you personally decide if something is beneficial when there are no specific commands for or against it in Scripture?

2. No one is perfect, so how can we be role models? How can we best handle the pressure of having others observe our lives? Should it even be a pressure situation? Why or why not?

3. In which gray areas do you have the hardest time discerning God's will? One way of deciding if something should be done is to ask yourself how the decision matches up with the character of God. How would knowing God better help in the area of integrity you struggle with?

Still More Influence: Have the women you are influencing answer this question; then have them do a theme study on the topics they chose, either as a team or as their homework assignment.

In which areas would you like more information on God's standards?

- ☐ marriage
- ☐ dating
- ☐ sex
- ☐ music
- ☐ dance
- ☐ alcohol
- ☐ friendships
- ☐ clothing/modesty
- ☐ food
- ☐ business
- ☐ extended family responsibilities
- ☐ money
- ☐ parenting

Chapter 8: A Woman of Influence Is Intense

1. Put yourself in Elijah's place. What step of restoration do you need to take? Why?

2. When are you most susceptible to burnout? (Idea: Have each group member create a TLC box or basket for another person; then exchange these at a group getaway or evening out.)

3. Prayer divides burdens. Spend an extended time praying for the concerns of those in your group.

Still More Influence: Sometimes we burn out because we are carrying more than God intended. Make a list of everything you are responsible for. Is there anything you can delegate or delete? Is there anything you can bring to closure or postpone? Study *sabbath* in the Bible. Maybe what you need is a short ministry break or change to get refreshed by God. Often, a more mature third party is a good sounding board during decision times like these. Even mentors need mentors!

Chapter 9: A Woman of Influence Is Inquiring

1. In what areas of life are you in a rut? What is something you can do today that would help you take one step out of the rut?

2. Think of a person who challenges you to grow spiritually. What does he or she do that stretches you? List five people you would like to spend time with because they stretch or challenge you. Call one of them and make an appointment.

3. Why does giving ourselves away help us grow? Think of the scariest places for you to minister. Why are those places scary to you? What can you do that would relieve some of that fear or prepare you to walk through that door or any door where God might ask you to go?

Still More Influence: As a woman of influence, you will find God increasing your platform for ministry as you seek to prepare to be your best for him wherever he calls. What areas of your personal or public ministry need to be strengthened? Where can you get the training needed? Seek out resources and choose one area to strengthen.

Chapter 10: A Woman of Influence Is Infectious

1. List natural connections you have with people who need Jesus (coworkers in volunteer groups, colleagues at work, neighbors). Get ideas from the group on how to strengthen and personalize those connections and influence those people for Jesus.

2. How do you feel about helping someone else grow in her faith and personal development? What obstacle(s) do you need to overcome in order to be more infectious as a leader?

3. Share your life purpose statement from "Living It Out." How can you be more effective in passing the baton of faith to this and future generations?

Still More Influence: Write a prayer to God, listing areas you'd like to grow in and asking his help. Put the prayer in an envelope addressed to yourself; seal and stamp it. Ask a friend to mail it to you after six months or a year. You may be amazed to see how God has worked!

Notes

Chapter 1: A Woman of Influence Is Impassioned

[1]Ruth Tucker and Walter Liefeld, *Daughters of the Church* (Grand Rapids, Mich.: Zondervan/Academie Books, 1987), p. 320.

[2]Christine Aroney-Sine, "The World's Women: A Call for Help," paper presented at Women's Ministries Symposium II, 1995. (For copies, contact Women's Ministries Institute, 1605 E. Elizabeth, Suite U-7, Pasadena, CA 91104.)

[3]William Bennett, *Index of Leading Cultural Indicators* (Washington, D.C.: Heritage Foundation, March 1993), pp. i-19.

[4]George Barna, *What Americans Believe* (Ventura, Calif.: Regal, 1991), p. 179.

[5]Chuck Swindoll, *Come Before Winter* (Portland, Ore.: Multnomah, 1985), p. 103.

[6]Elizabeth Mittelstaedt, "Living by God's Promises," *Today's Christian Woman*, Jan.-Feb. 1995, p. 72.

[7]Tucker and Liefeld, *Daughters of the Church, p. 192.*

[8]A. Wetherell Johnson, *Created for Commitment* (Wheaton, Ill.: Tyndale, 1982), pp. 136-37.

[9]Tucker and Liefeld, *Daughters of the Church*, p. 102.

[10]Robert Bolt, *A Man for All Seasons* (New York: Vintage Books, 1960), p. 81.

[11]Edith Deen, *Great Women of the Christian Faith* (New York: Harper, 1959), p. 216.

[12]Ibid.

Chapter 2: A Woman of Influence Is an Individual

[1]Maureen Sajbel, "Hat Tricks," *Los Angeles Times,* July 14, 1994, p. E3.

[2]Jennifer Levitz, "Cancer Patients Hold Their Heads High," *Times Advocate,*

Aug. 23, 1995, p. A1.

[3]Sally Helgesen, *The Female Advantage: Women's Ways of Leadership* (New York: Doubleday, 1990), pp. 19-28.

[4]Gary N. Powell, *Women and Men in Management* (Newbury Park, Calif.: Sage Publications, 1993), p. 167.

[5]Ibid., p. 84.

[6]See ibid., p. 162, for gender differences. Several studies showed men's aspirations and self-perception of leadership skills as higher than women's (see pp. 76-79, 105-6).

[7]Ibid., p. 109.

[8]Ibid., p. 107.

[9]Julie A. Talerico, "Elizabeth Dole's Heart and Soul," *Today's Christian Woman*, July-Aug. 1993, p. 78.

[10]Johnson, *Created for Commitment*, p. 46.

[11]Tucker and Liefeld, *Daughters of the Church*, p. 271.

[12]Anne Graham Lotz, "Women in Ministry," audiotape available from AnGeL Ministry, P.O. Box 31167, Raleigh, NC 27622-1167.

[13]Jill Briscoe, "Woman Power: The Woman's Place in the Church," audiotape 0988-8, available from Telling the Truth Ministries, P.O. Box 11, Brookfield, WI 53008.

[14]Ruth Tucker, in a personal conversation, Women's Ministry Symposium, Mar. 24, 1995.

[15]Source unknown. Excerpted from *Hope for the Heart* newsletter, Dec. 1992 (P.O. Box 7, Dallas, TX 75221).

[16]Fern Nichols, in a personal interview, Jan. 9, 1995.

Chapter 3: A Woman of Influence Is Intimate with God

[1]C. S. Lewis, *The Screwtape Letters* (Old Tappan, N.J.: Revell, 1979), p. 59.

[2]Nancy Carmichael, "Any Bush Will Do," *Virtue*, Jan.-Feb. 1994, p. 31.

[3]"The Quilters," *Virtue*, Mar.-Apr. 1991, p. 44.

[4]Nancy Mankins, New Tribes Mission audiotape, Mar. 16, 1993.

[5]*Shadowlands*, film directed and produced by Richard Attenborough, 1993. HBO Home Video and Savoy Video production. Also produced by Brian Eastman, 1993.

[6]*1 to 1 Discipleship Manual* (Vista, Calif.: Church Dynamics, 1983), p. 24.

[7]Teresa Muller, "You Are the Rock of My Salvation," *Praise VII*, © 1982, Maranatha Music. Used by permission.

Chapter 4: A Woman of Influence Is Idealistic

[1]Earl O. Roe, *Dream Big* (Ventura, Calif.: Regal, 1990), p. 265.

[2]Ibid., p. 161.

[3]Ibid., p. 57.

[4]Paraphrased from 1 Chronicles 29:11-12; Job 41:33; Psalm 139; Isaiah 9:6; 40; Zechariah 4:6; Matthew 17:20; Romans 8:38-40; 11:33; Ephesians 3:20; Colossians 1:16-17; 1 Timothy 6:16; Hebrews 4:16; Revelation 22:13.

[5]R. V. J. Tasker, *The Second Epistle of Paul to the Corinthians*, Tyndale New Testament Commentaries 8 (London: Inter-Varsity Press, 1983), p. 49.

[6]Quoted in Deen, *Great Women of the Christian Faith*, p. 269.

[7]William Brooks, "Mary, Queen of Calabar," *Worldwide Challenge*, July-Aug. 1994, p. 47.

[8]William Bennett, *The Book of Virtues* (New York: Simon & Schuster, 1993), pp. 503-4.

[9]Paul Thigpen, "Harriet Tubman: Risking Her Life to Set Others Free," *Discipleship Journal, Nov.-Dec. 1994, p. 63.*

Chapter 5: A Woman of Influence Is Interdependent

[1]Vonette Bright, *The Greatest Lesson* (San Bernardino, Calif.: Here's Life Publishers, 1990), p. 174.

[2]InfoSearch, NavPress PC Software, illustration 62.

[3]Elisabeth Elliot, *A Chance to Die* (Grand Rapids, Mich.: Revell, 1987), p. 15.

[4]Elizabeth Cody Newenhuyse, "Friendship Fizzle," *Today's Christian Woman,* Jan.-Feb. 1995, p. 52.

Chapter 6: A Woman of Influence Takes Initiative

[1]Deen, *Great Women of the Christian Faith,* p. 243.

[2]Ibid., p. 239.

[3]Emilie Barnes, *The Creative Home Organizer* (Eugene, Ore.: Harvest House, 1988), p. 15.

[4]Patrick Marley, *Man in the Mirror* (Brentwood, Tenn.: Wolgemuth & Hyatt, 1989), p. 84.

[5]Daisy Hepburn, address given at women's conference, Pine Valley, Calif., Mar. 11, 1989.

[6]Corrie ten Boom, *Each New Day* (Grand Rapids, Mich.: Spire, 1977), p. 39.

[7]Excellent financial resources are available at your local Christian bookstore. Authors include Ron and Judy Blue and Larry Burkett.

[8]Jack Canfield and Mark Hansen, *Chicken Soup for the Soul* (Deerfield Beach, Fla.: Health Communications, 1993), pp. 228-30.

Chapter 7: A Woman of Influence Has Integrity

[1]Robert Logan, *Beyond Church Growth* (Grand Rapids, Mich.: Revell, 1989), p. 38, quoting James Kouzes and Barry Posner in *The Leadership Challenge* (San Francisco, Calif.: Jossey-Bass, 1987), pp. 15-27

[2]For more information on spiritual warfare and your identity in Christ, contact Freedom in Christ Ministries, 491 East Lambert Rd., La Habra, CA 90631. Phone (310) 691-9128.

[3]InfoSearch, illustration 1927.

[4]Clark Cothen, "To Illustrate," *Honesty, Leadership,* Fall 1994, p. 43.

Chapter 8: A Woman of Influence Is Intense

[1]Kenny Moore, "Dash to Glory," *Sports Illustrated,* Aug. 10, 1992, p. 18.

[2]"Devers Overcomes Ailments to Dash for Olympic Gold," *Jet,* Aug. 17, 1992, p. 51.

[3]Moore, 'Dash to Glory," p. 19.

[4]"Devers Overcomes Ailments," p. 51.

[5]Ibid., p. 25.

[6]Deniese George, "Capturing a Nation's Heart," *Pursuit* 11, no. 4, p. 26.

[7]Ibid., p. 30.

[8]"Heather Whitestone," *People,* Dec. 26, 1994, p. 122.

[9]Jill Briscoe, "Running on Empty" audiotape. 1991 National Conference for Ministry Wives, Feb. 19-21, 1991, Orlando, Fla.

[10]Neil Taylor, *How to Lose 10 Pounds* (Nashville, Tenn.: Nelson, 1993), p. 37.

[11]Deen, *Great Women of the Christian Faith,* p. 78.

[12]Jill Briscoe, Newim Conference, June 2, 1994, Arrowhead Springs, Calif.

[13]Walvoord and Zuck, *Bible Knowledge Commentary,* p. 527.

[14]Neil Anderson, Freedom in Christ Seminar, San Diego, Calif., July 1994.

[15]Stormie Omartian, *Greater Health God's Way* (Chatsworth, Calif.: Sparrow, 1984), p. 52.

Chapter 9: A Woman of Influence Is Inquiring

[1]Chuck Colson, *Loving God* (Grand Rapids, Mich.: Zondervan, 1983), pp. 209-16.

[2]InfoSearch, illustration 109.

[3]Charlie Jones and Bob Phillips, *Wit and Wisdom* (Eugene, Ore.: Harvest House, 1977), p. 52.

[4]Ibid., p. 53.

[5]Logan, *Beyond Church Growth,* p. 42.

Chapter 10: A Woman of Influence Is Infectious

[1]Edith Wharton, in "Quotable Quotes," *Reader's Digest,* Aug. 1994, p. 29.

[2]Cynthia McKinney, in a personal interview, Dec. 12, 1994.

[3]Lonni Collins Pratt, "Charla Pereau: Springs of Faith in a Desert," *Discipleship Journal,* Nov.-Dec. 1994, p. 43.

[4]Monica Whiting, "Living Christ and Gabbing over Lunch," *Discipleship*

Journal, Sept.-Oct. 1994, p. 41.

[5]Kay Cole James, *Never Forget* (Grand Rapids, Mich.: Zondervan, 1992), p. 159.

[6]Ibid., p. 169.

[7]Robert Coleman, *The Master Plan of Evangelism* (Old Tappan, N.J.: Spire, 1978), p. 24.

Pam Farrel is a director of women's ministries, a pastor's wife and a freelance writer and speaker. She is the author of numerous articles in newspapers and magazines, including a Focus on the Family publication. Pam is also coauthor of *Pure Pleasure: Making Your Marriage a Great Affair* (IVP), written with her husband, Bill, and Jim and Sally Conway. She is the mother of three children. To contact Pam, write to her at Masterful Living, 629 S. Rancho Santa Fe, San Marcos, CA 92069. Or phone (619) 727-9122.